D0568185

ART CENTER COLLEGE OF DESIGN
3 3220 00134 3198

The Body

CONTENTS

LOOKING CLOSER 4
INTRODUCTION 5
SKIN AND HAIR 6
MUSCLE AND BONE 8
BLOOD AND BLOOD VESSELS 10
LUNGS AND BREATHING 12
THE DIGESTIVE SYSTEM 14
THE EXCRETORY SYSTEM 16
THE NERVOUS SYSTEM 18
EYES AND EARS 20
THE REPRODUCTIVE SYSTEM 22
THE EMBRYO 24
BODY DEFENSES AND ATTACKERS 26
PRACTICAL PROJECTS 28
MICROPHOTOGRAPHY 30
GLOSSARY 31

Designed and produced by
Aladdin Books Ltd
70 Old Compton Street
London W1

Design David West
Children's Book Design
Author Lionel Bender
Editor Roger Vlitos
Researcher C. Weston-Baker
Illustrated by Alex Pang

First published in the United States in 1989 by
Gloucester Press
387 Park Avenue South
New York, NY 10016

Printed in Belgium

Library of Congress Cataloging-in-Publication Data
Bender, Lionel
p. cm The body / (Through the microscope)
Includes Index Summary: Text and microscopic photographs introduce the parts of the human body, including internal organs, systems and other aspects of human physiology.
ISBN 0-531-17183-3
1. Human physiology - Juvenile literature. 2. Body, Human - Juvenile literature. [1. Body, Human 2. Human physiology.]
I Title. II. Series
QP37.B46 1989
612--dc20

89-31786
CIP
AC

THROUGH · THE · MICROSCOPE

The Body

GLOUCESTER PRESS
New York · London · Toronto · Sydney

LOOKING CLOSER

Microscopes and magnifying glasses work by using lenses and light. A lens is usually a thin, circular glass, thicker in the middle, which bends rays of light so that when you look through it an object appears enlarged. A microscope uses several lenses. It will also have a set of adjustments to give you a choice of how much you want to magnify.

When we want to view something under a microscope it must be small enough to fit on a glass slide. This is put on the stage over the mirror and light is reflected through so that the lenses inside can magnify the view for us. But not all microscopes work this way. The greatest detail can be seen with an electron microscope which uses electron beams and electromagnets.

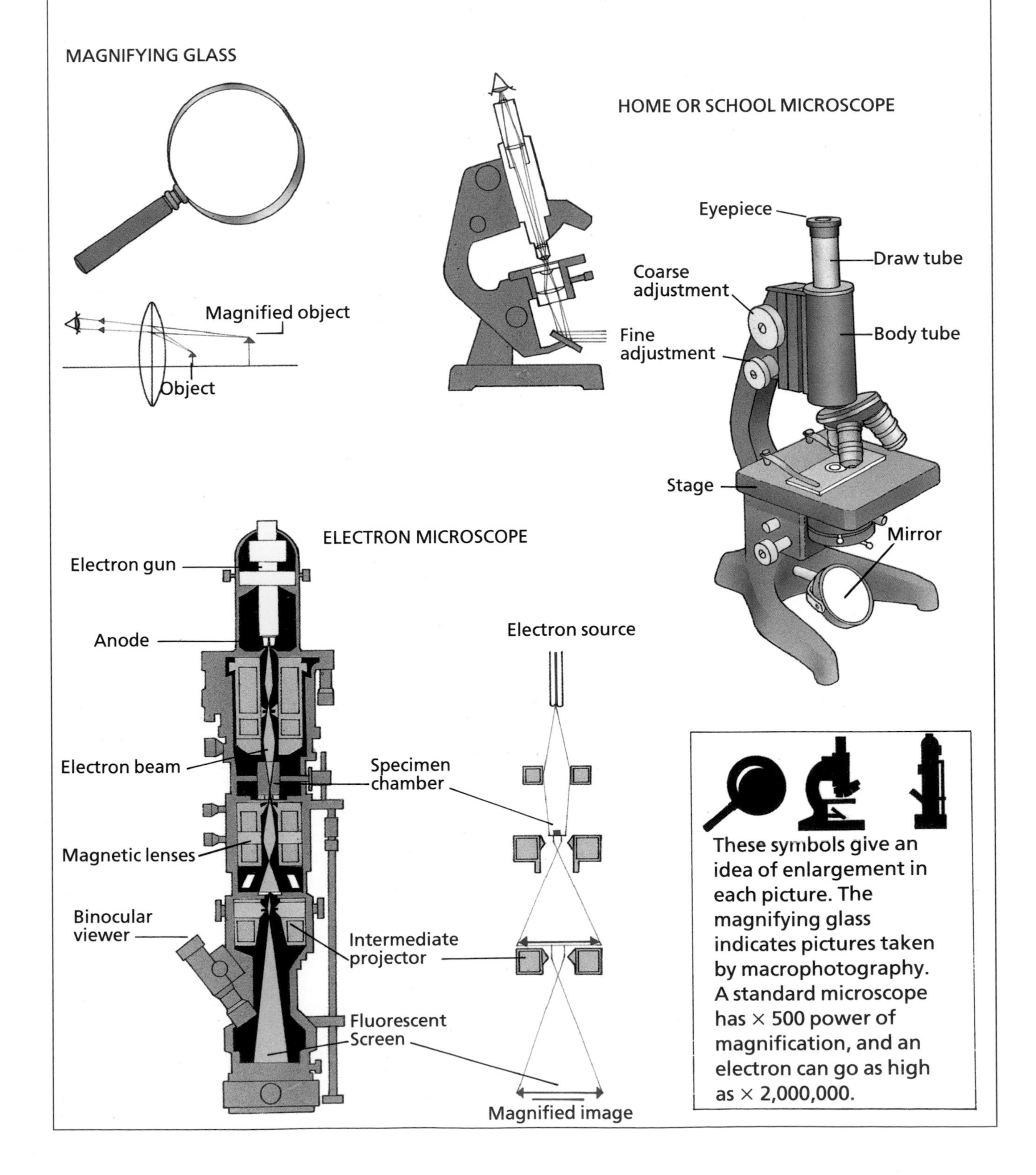

These symbols give an idea of enlargement in each picture. The magnifying glass indicates pictures taken by macrophotography. A standard microscope has × 500 power of magnification, and an electron can go as high as × 2,000,000.

INTRODUCTION

A microscope is used to study things too small to be seen with the naked eye. This book has pictures taken through microscopes, or with special magnifying lenses attached to cameras. Drawings appear alongside to help explain what the microscopes are showing us.

The human body is made up of tiny building units called cells, which are only about 0.03mm (0.0001in) wide, but grow together to form skin, nerves, bone, and even hair. In this book we look in turn at the body systems shown below to reveal the beauty and complexity of each.

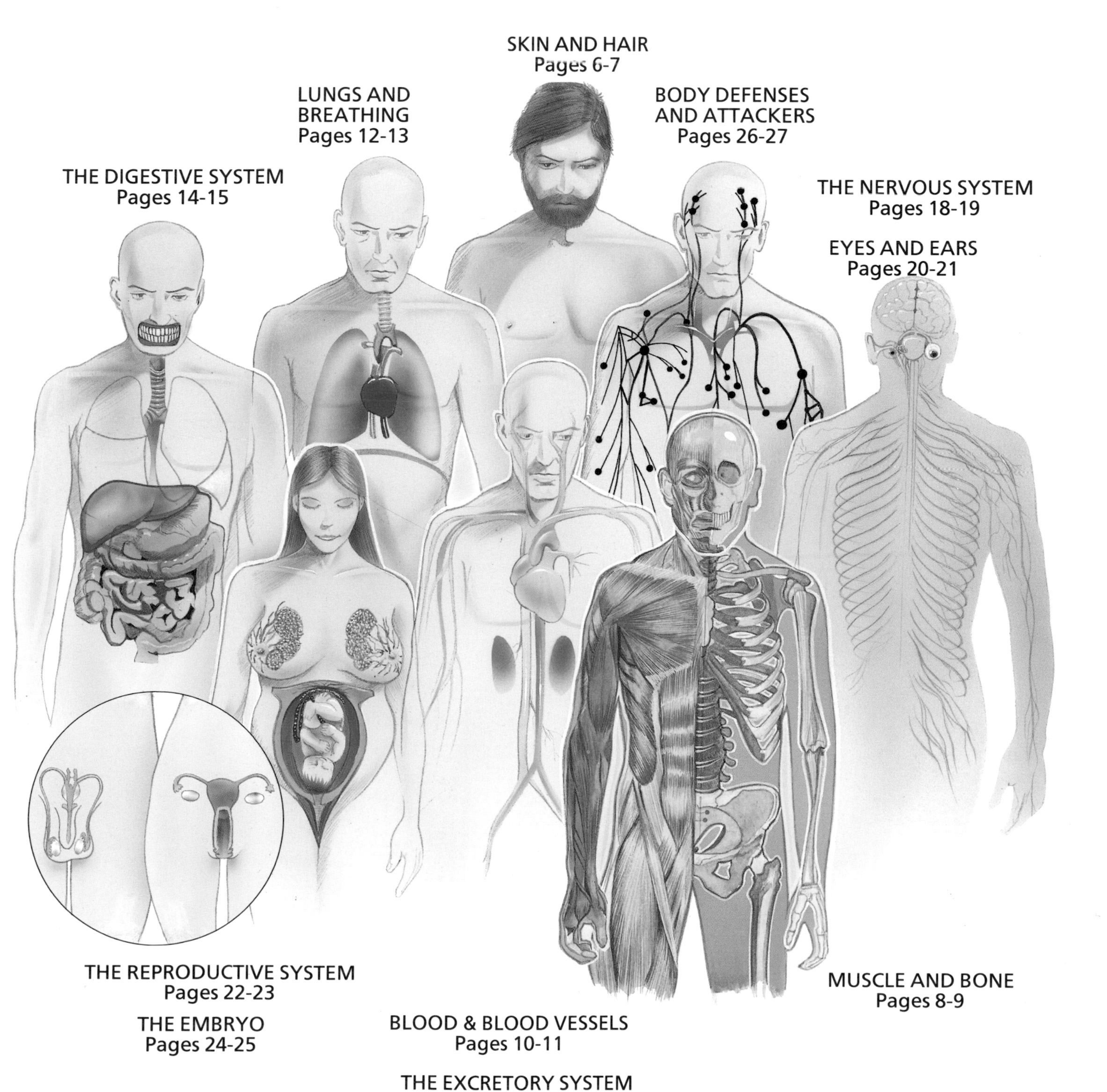

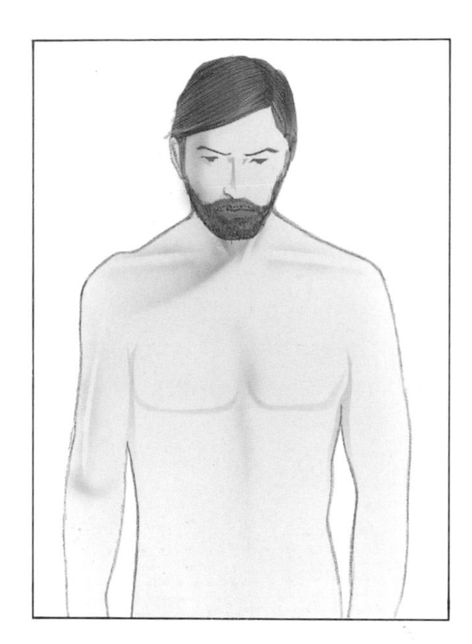

SKIN AND HAIR

Skin covers our bodies and cushions the soft tissues beneath from injury and attack by germs. With just a magnifying glass you can see two layers of skin, the epidermis on top and the dermis underneath. The epidermis consists of hard, dead cells that fit together tightly like paving stones on a path. These get worn away every day as we wash, dress, and move around. But they are always being replaced by new skin cells rising from the dermis below. Except on the palms of your hands and the soles of your feet the skin is covered with hairs. They grow from pits in the dermis and seen through an electron microscope, below, resemble trees rising in rings from their follicle, or growing-pit.

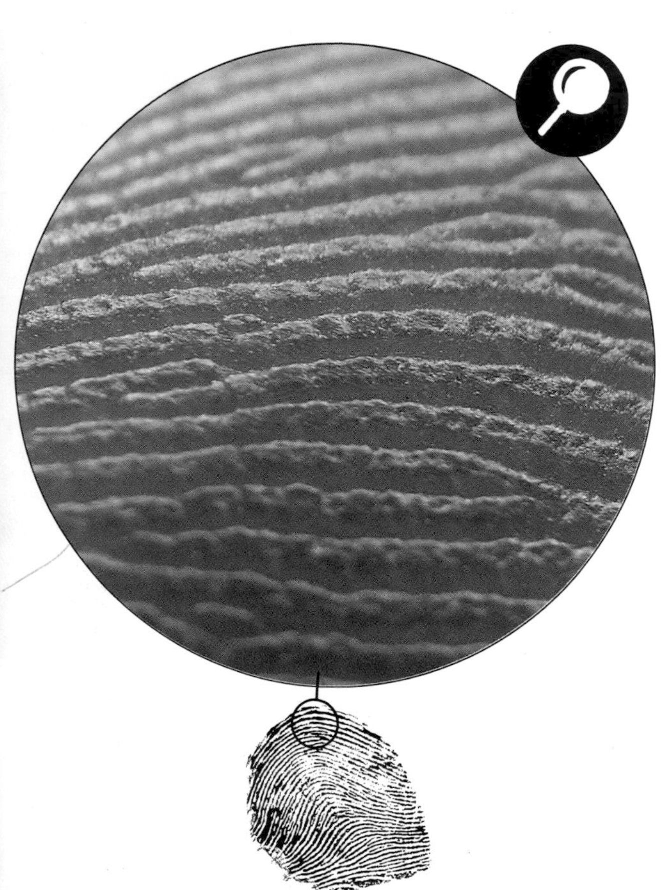

A fingerprint is a pattern of tiny ridges in the skin. No two fingerprints are ever the same. You can find such ridges on your hands and feet where they are needed for grip. Over the rest of your body the skin is smoother and thinner as it has to put up with less wear and tear. The skin on your palms, for instance,is 100 times thicker than on your face.

These two human hairs look like strange creatures, and in a way they are. Hairs can continue to grow even after a person dies.

Various structures are embedded in the dermis of the skin (see illustration left). The temperature, touch, pain, and pressure nerves are there; and oil glands to keep the epidermis (or surface) from getting dry and flaky. Hairs grow from pits called follicles. Each hair is a tube of dead epidermal cells filled with a chemical called keratin. When one falls out it is usually replaced by another which grows from a root in the follicle. The skin also has sweat glands which make a watery fluid that seeps out of tiny holes called pores. There are over two million of these to help keep the body cool when it gets too hot. The picture on the bottom right of this page shows just one of these from a man's palm.

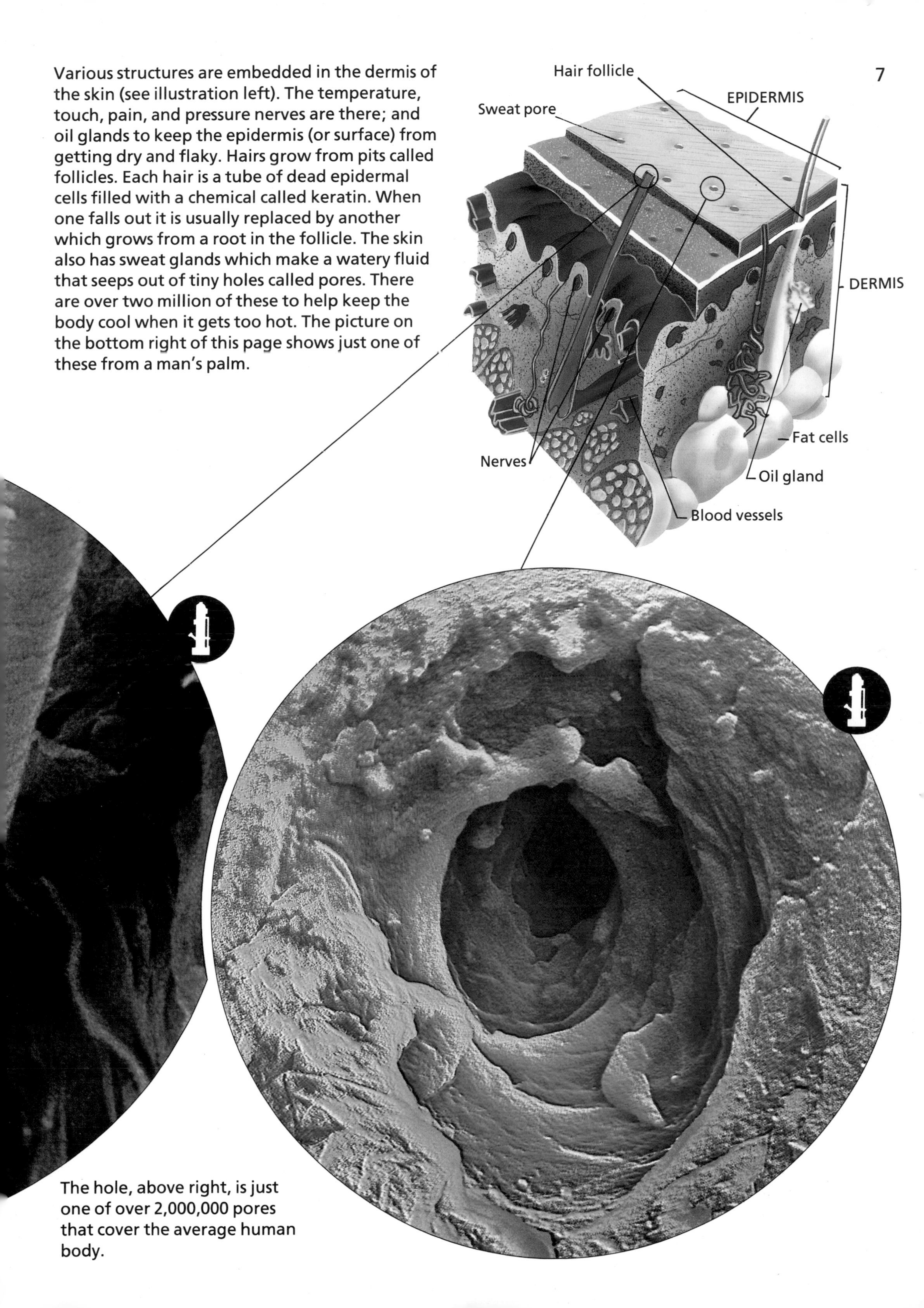

The hole, above right, is just one of over 2,000,000 pores that cover the average human body.

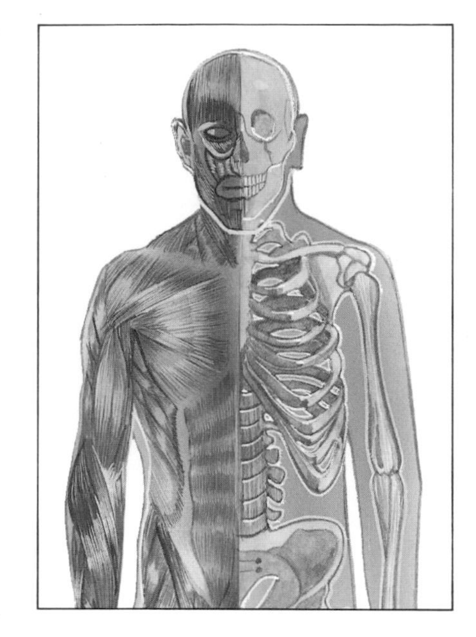

MUSCLE AND BONE

There are over 650 muscles in your body. A muscle is a fleshy bundle of fibers usually attached to a bone. Every movement we make is the work of muscles. Even your heartbeat is a muscular action. When you move an arm or leg, one muscle shortens to pull two bones closer while another muscle relaxes to let it go. About 200 bones form the skeleton which supports your body. Its most important organs, like the brain and the heart, are protected by the skull and rib bones. Bones have a hard, white coating but are almost hollow. They are filled with marrow which makes most of the blood cells for your body. Far from being dry and brittle objects, bones are living structures.

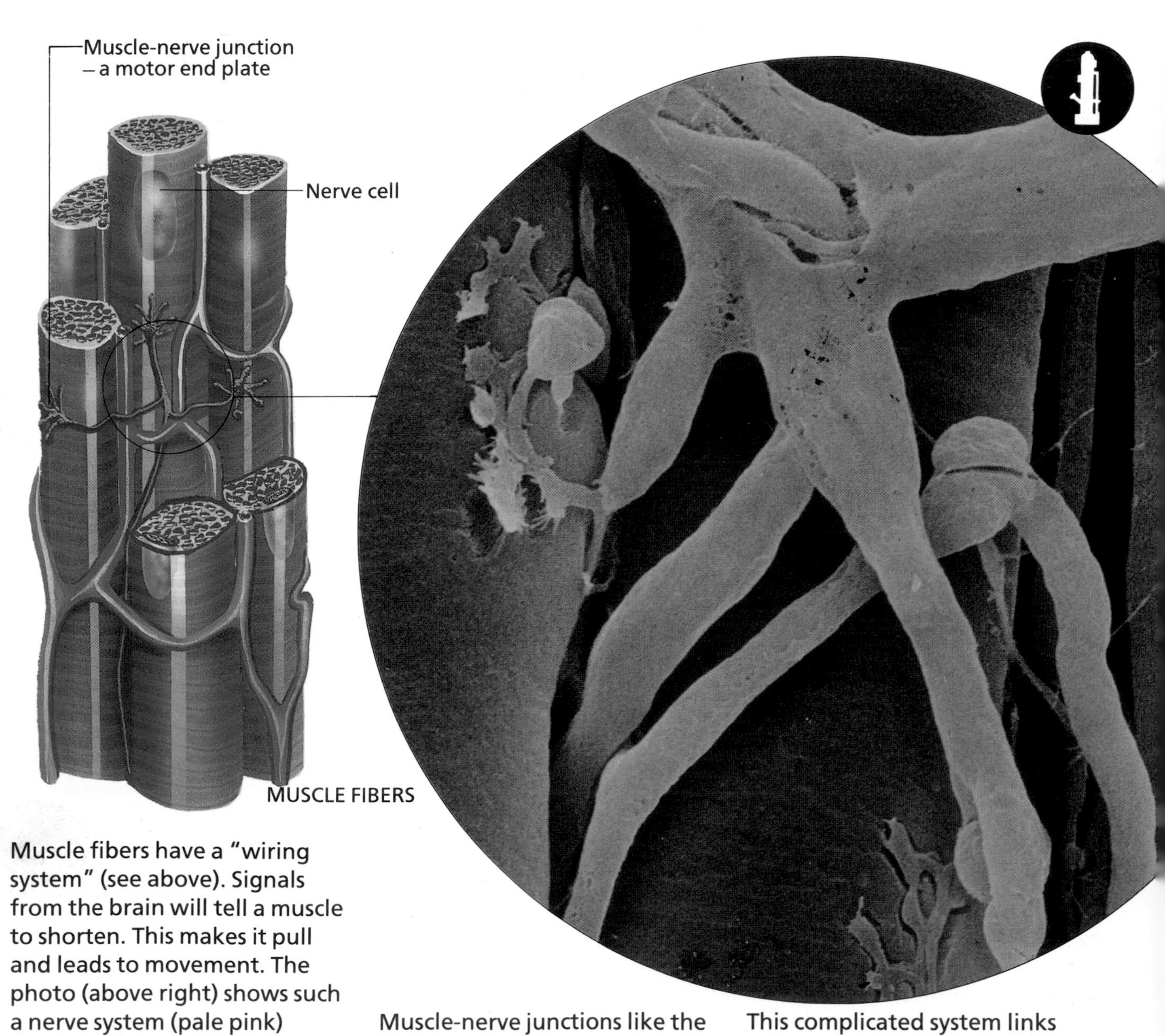

Muscle fibers have a "wiring system" (see above). Signals from the brain will tell a muscle to shorten. This makes it pull and leads to movement. The photo (above right) shows such a nerve system (pale pink) connected to muscle fibers by two motor end plates.

Muscle-nerve junctions like the one pictured above are repeated all over your body.

This complicated system links every muscle movement to the brain.

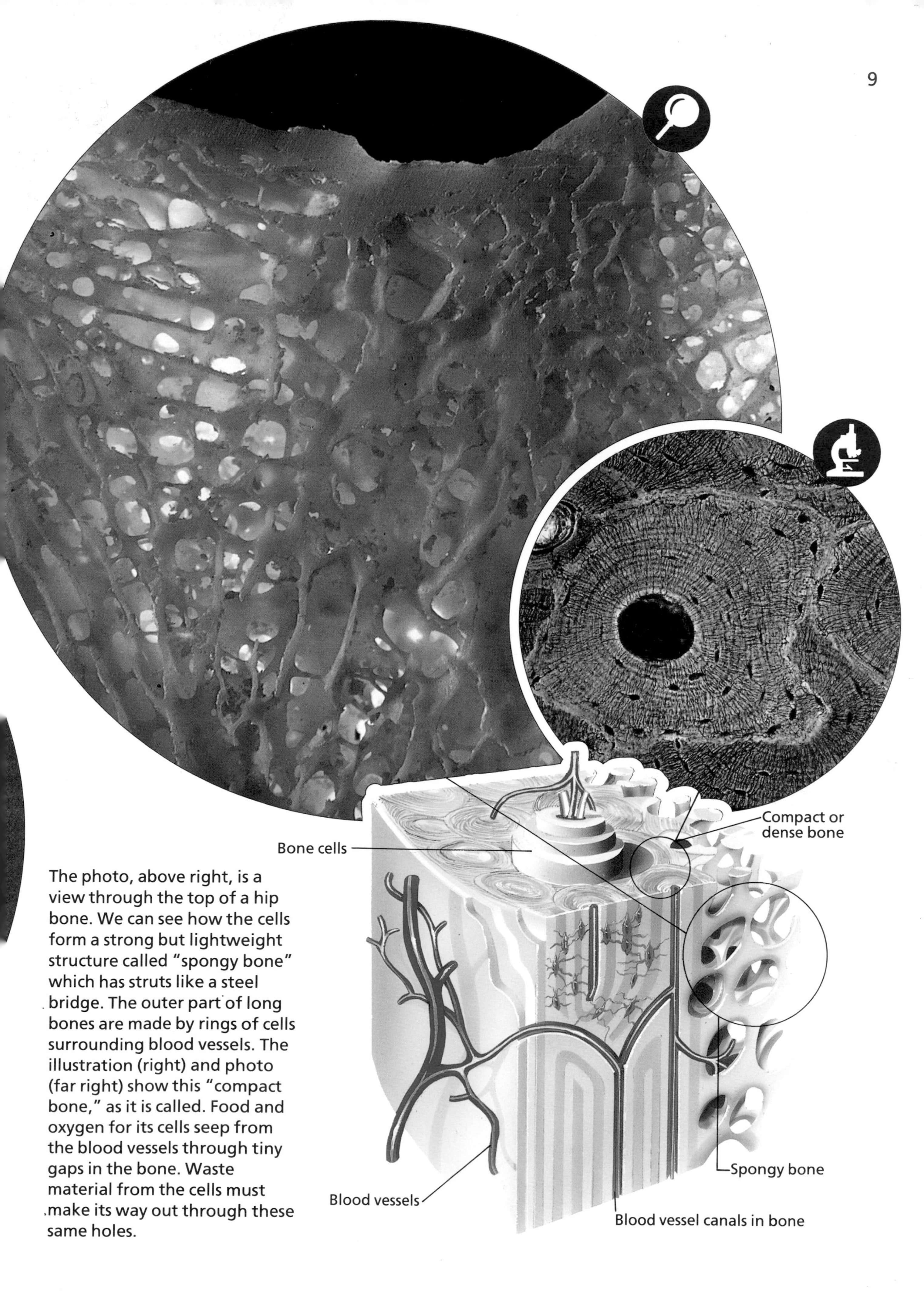

The photo, above right, is a view through the top of a hip bone. We can see how the cells form a strong but lightweight structure called "spongy bone" which has struts like a steel bridge. The outer part of long bones are made by rings of cells surrounding blood vessels. The illustration (right) and photo (far right) show this "compact bone," as it is called. Food and oxygen for its cells seep from the blood vessels through tiny gaps in the bone. Waste material from the cells must make its way out through these same holes.

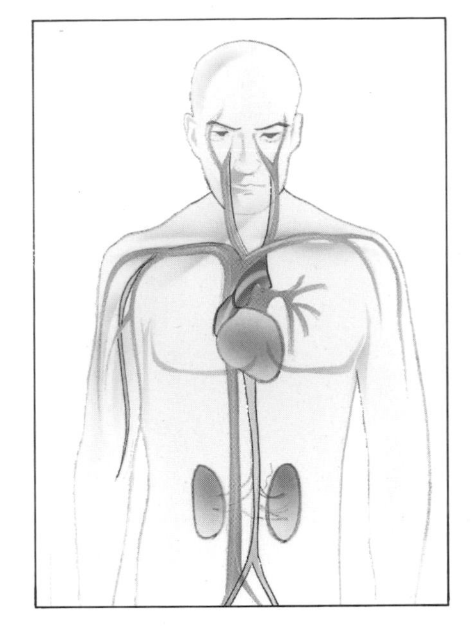

BLOOD AND BLOOD VESSELS

Our hearts are continually pumping blood through the 80,000 kilometers, or 50,000 miles, of blood vessels in our bodies (see illustration left). Blood circulates within the body and carries food materials, heat, and special chemicals called hormones to all our tissues and organs. It also takes away waste products like carbon dioxide and urea, to be dealt with by other main organs. Under a microscope we can see that blood consists of a yellowish, sticky fluid called plasma which has red and white cells called corpuscles. The red blood cells are colored by hemoglobin, which carries oxygen from the lungs to the tissues. White cells attack and destroy germs whenever they enter the bloodstream.

The largest vessels of the blood system are the veins and arteries. The smallest are capillaries (see illustration below). The widest artery is only about 2cm (¾in) across, but this quickly divides into smaller arterioles. Blood flows through these and into tiny capillary "nets" within tissues. These are only 0.007mm, or a fraction of an inch wide. Here red cells tumble freely through while the white cells , which are much larger, have to squeeze by. The picture on the right shows red cells packed into a blood capillary.

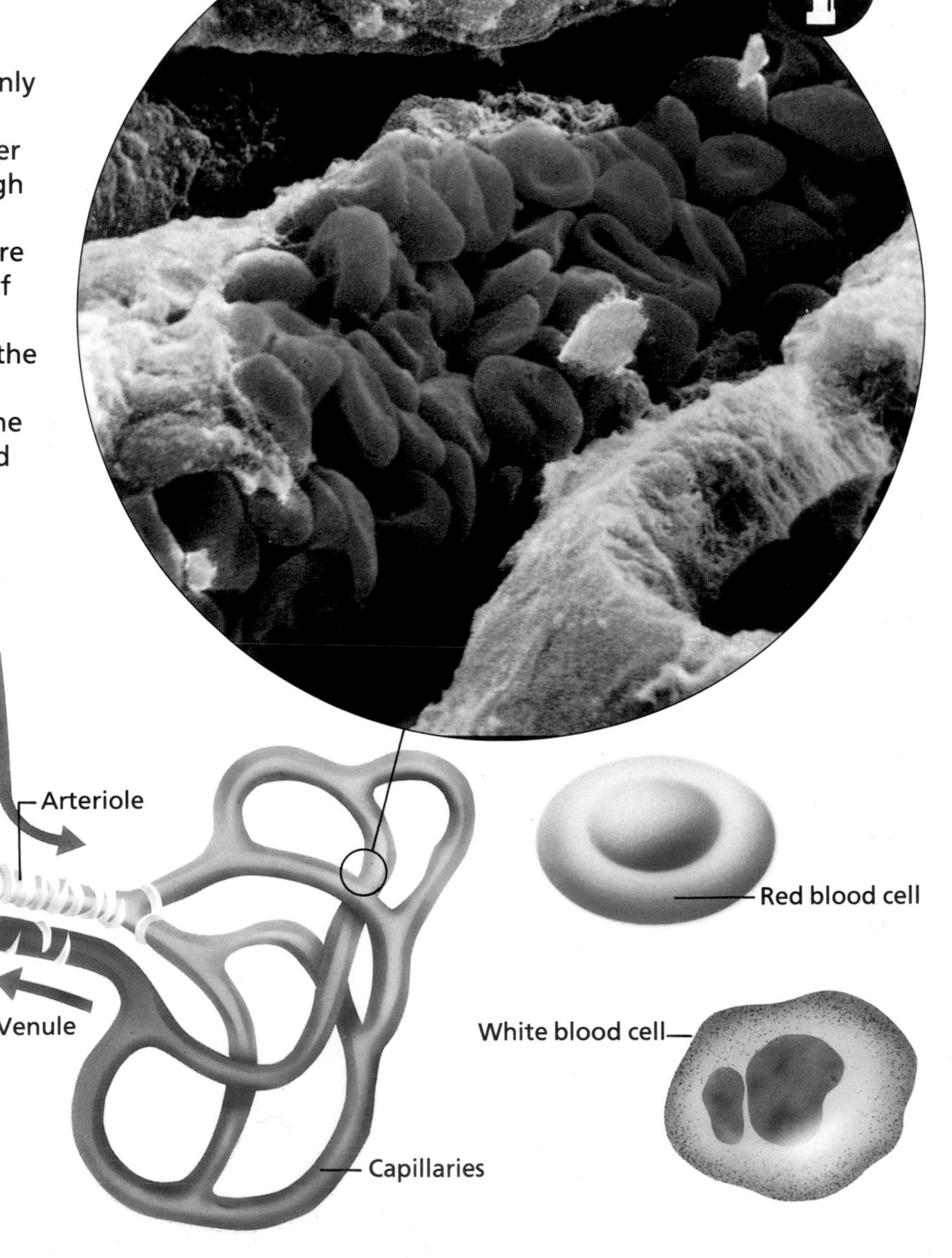

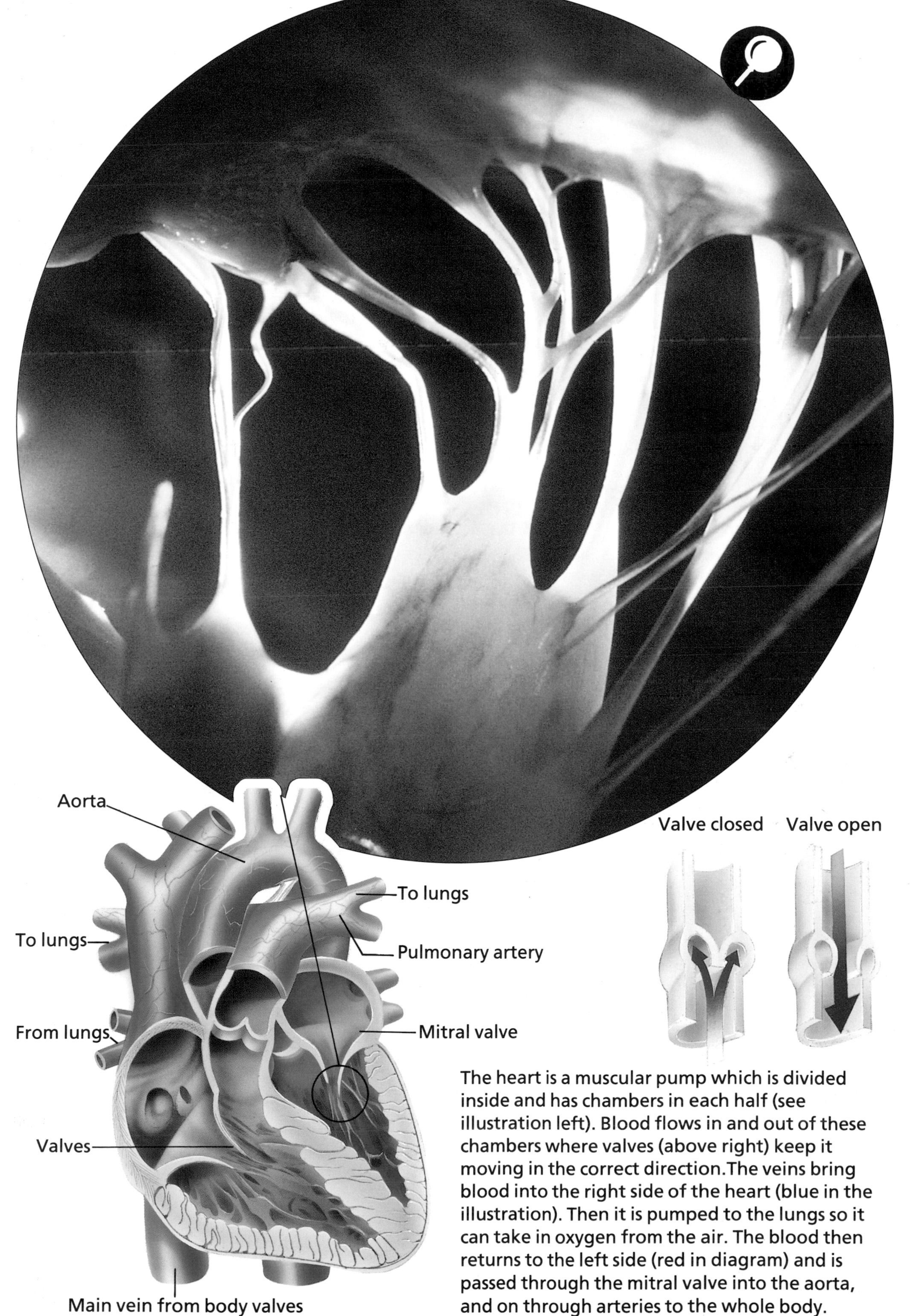

The heart is a muscular pump which is divided inside and has chambers in each half (see illustration left). Blood flows in and out of these chambers where valves (above right) keep it moving in the correct direction.The veins bring blood into the right side of the heart (blue in the illustration). Then it is pumped to the lungs so it can take in oxygen from the air. The blood then returns to the left side (red in diagram) and is passed through the mitral valve into the aorta, and on through arteries to the whole body.

LUNGS AND BREATHING

Every cell in your body needs oxygen and without it each would die in only 4 minutes. Oxygen helps change our food into energy. However, at the same time, a waste gas called carbon dioxide is produced which we need to get rid of. The lungs are the organs which deal with the exchange of these two gases. They are made of millions of air sacs surrounded by capillaries full of blood. Each time we breathe in, they expand like balloons and allow oxygen to pass through their thin walls into the bloodstream. When we breathe out, they contract so that the carbon dioxide waste is expelled. Whenever your body needs more oxygen, when you are running, for example, you start breathing more quickly and deeply.

Hairs line the inside of the nose and are covered in a sticky fluid called mucus. These hairs trap any dust and germs which may enter when you breathe in. Air gets into the lungs through a tree-like arrangement of pipes.

The trachea, or windpipe, is like the trunk. This is lined with yellow, grass-like cilia (photo below). The windpipe branches into tiny twigs within each lung called bronchioles. See illustration on the right.

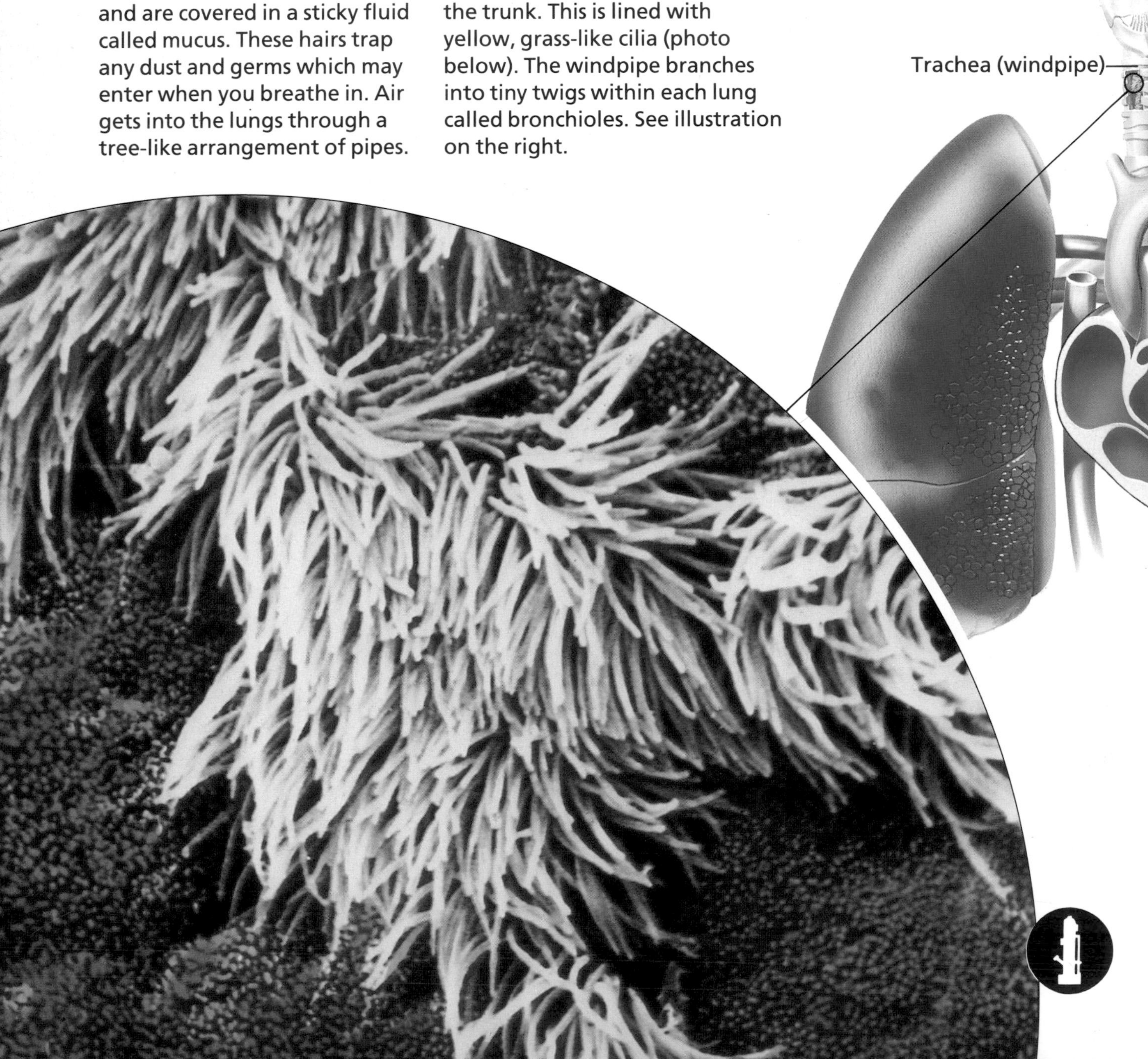

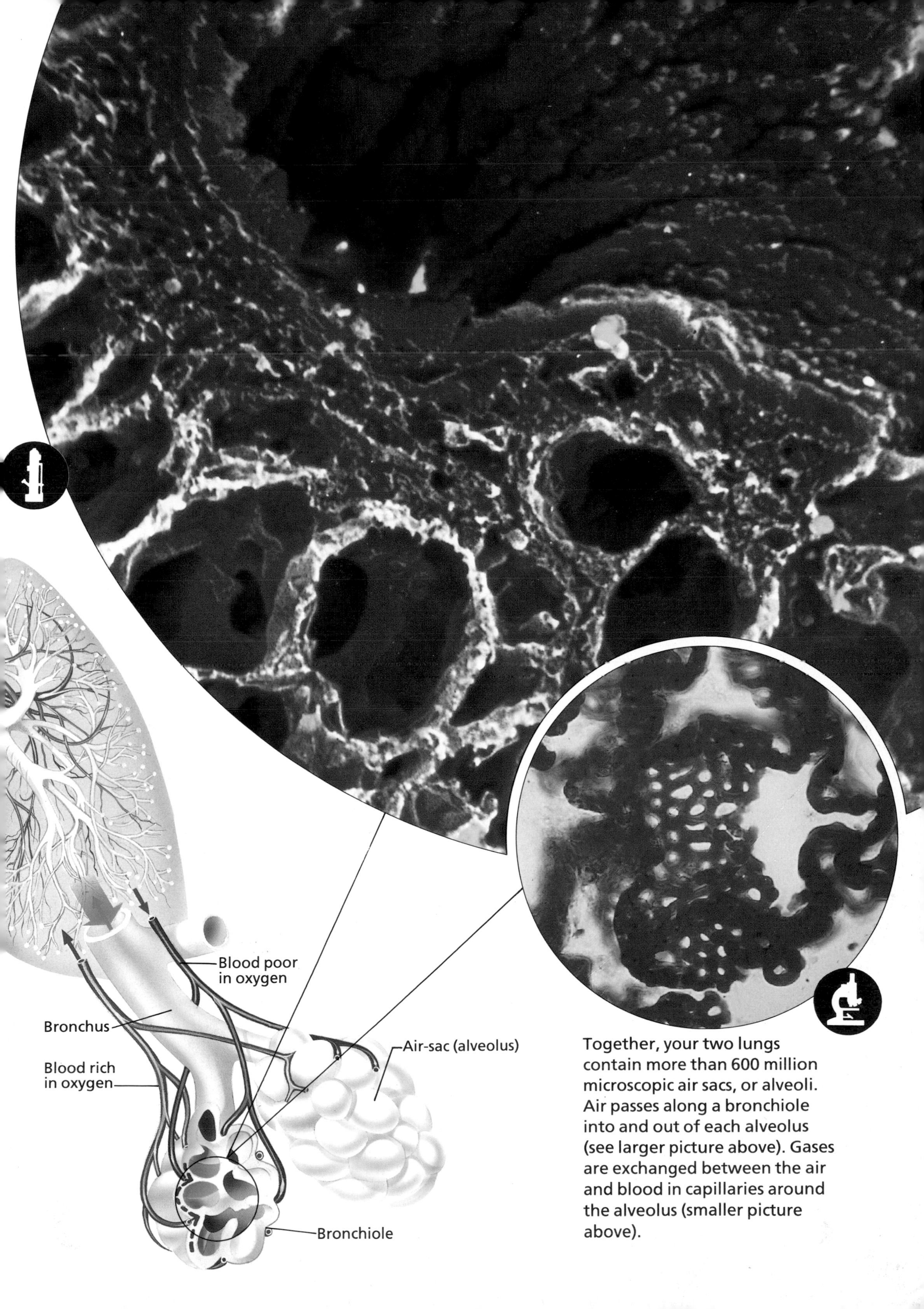

Together, your two lungs contain more than 600 million microscopic air sacs, or alveoli. Air passes along a bronchiole into and out of each alveolus (see larger picture above). Gases are exchanged between the air and blood in capillaries around the alveolus (smaller picture above).

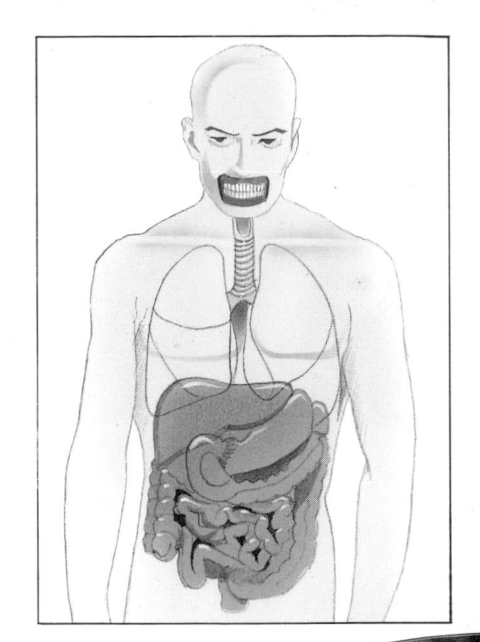

THE DIGESTIVE SYSTEM

The human body is like a machine built from, and fueled with, food. But for our cells to use the food, it must first be converted into simple chemicals which will enter the bloodstream and so travel to where they are needed. This is the job of our digestive system. Think of it as a seven meter (23 ft) long tube winding through your body, changing food into fuel. First food is softened in your mouth by chewing. Once swallowed, it is attacked by acids in your stomach and intestines until it is so broken-down that the chemicals can pass through the walls of the tube (or digestive tract) into the blood, or lymph system. Finally, whatever the body cannot digest is excreted as feces.

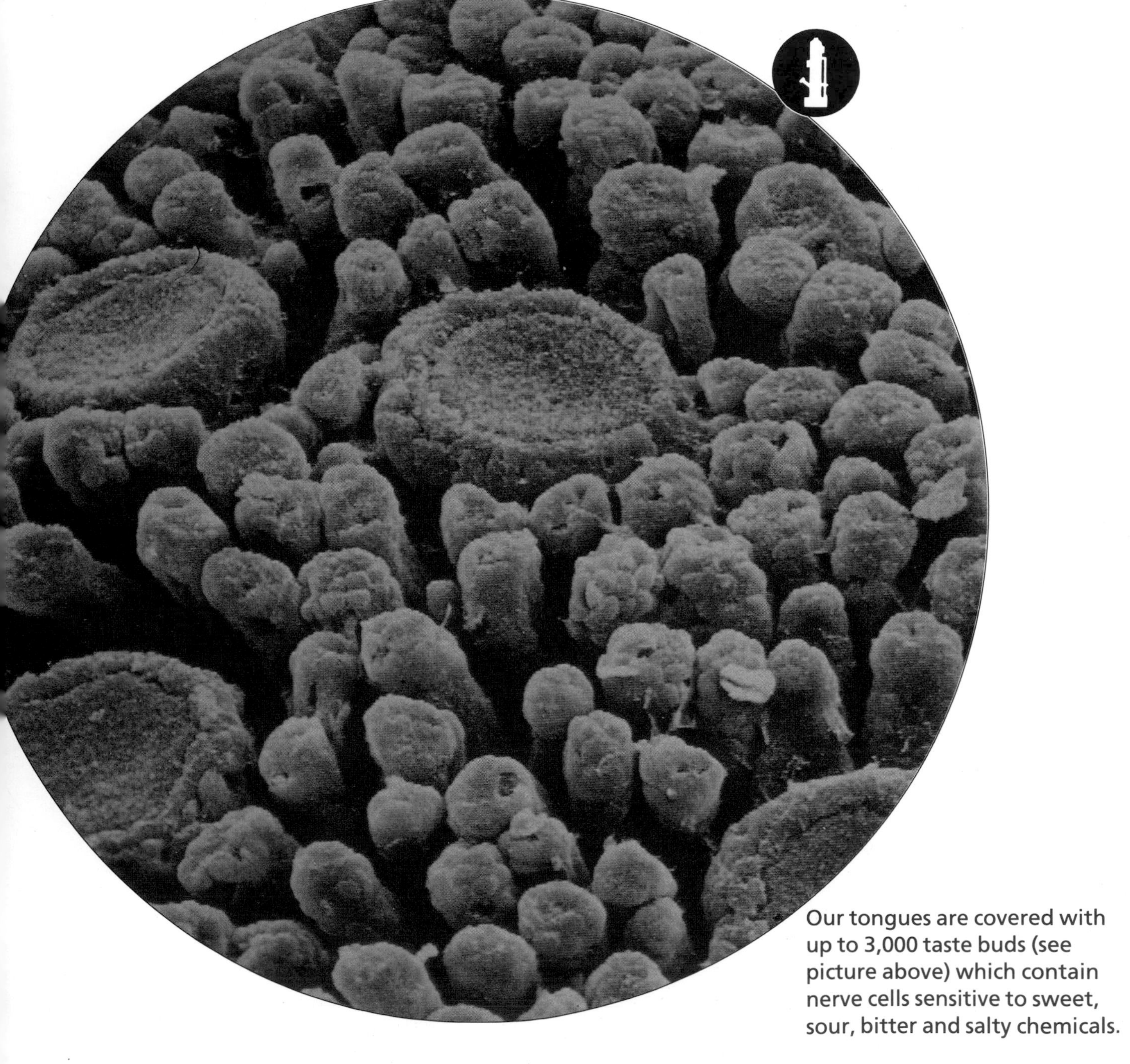

Our tongues are covered with up to 3,000 taste buds (see picture above) which contain nerve cells sensitive to sweet, sour, bitter and salty chemicals.

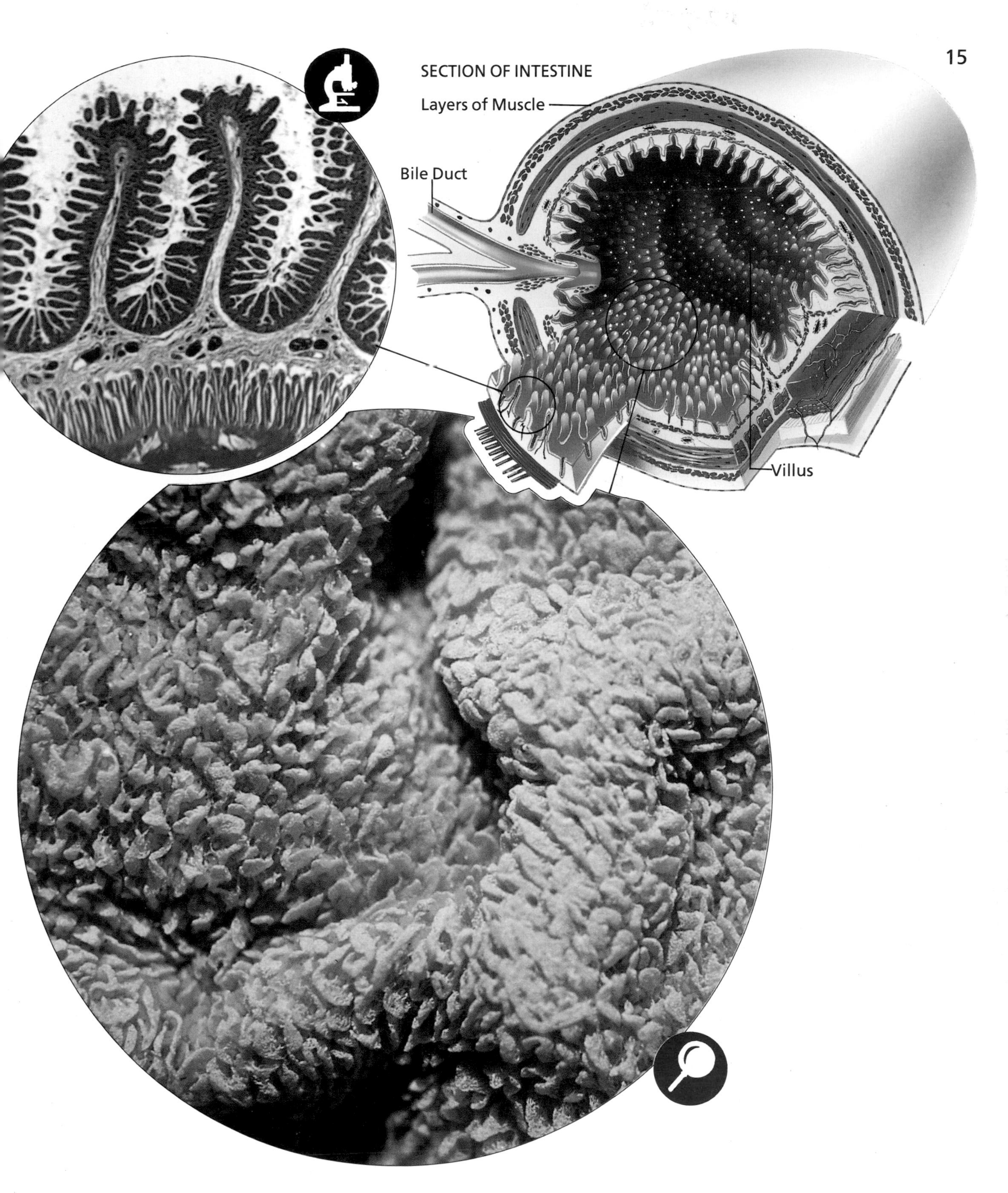

Each day , your digestive system will handle about 10 liters, or 18 pints, of food and drink from your stomach and intestines. Only about 125ml, less than one pint, of this leaves your body as feces. The rest is absorbed into capillaries and lymph vessels in the walls of the intestines (see photo and illustration uppermost on this page). Most absorption takes place in the duodenum (photo above). The walls of your intestines are so highly folded that they have a surface area that would be larger than a tennis court if they were to be spread out flat.

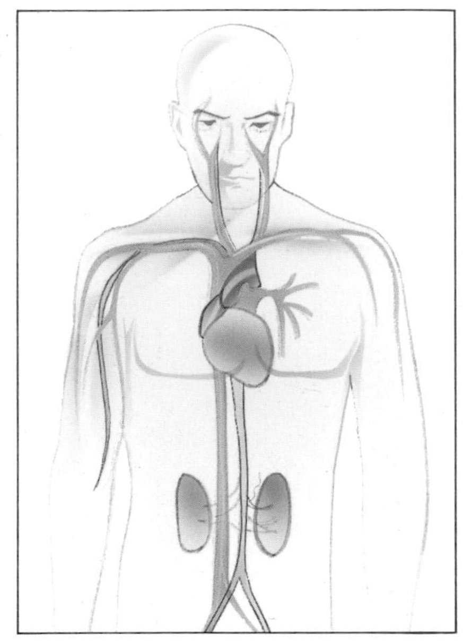

THE EXCRETORY SYSTEM

Your blood contains many substances that the body does not need and a few that can actually be harmful to you. These include excess water and minerals from food, dead or damaged cells, and waste products of cell activity. They must be eliminated from your body if you are to stay healthy. Your kidneys are the organs that filter your blood and remove the chemicals and water.One quarter of all the blood your heart pumps is sent straight to your kidneys. This means that every day your heart pumps about 1,500 liters of blood through your kidneys. Small materials are squeezed out of blood capillaries into microscopic filter units to form a trickle of unwanted water and waste products known as urine.

Each kidney contains a million filter units called nephrons. At the top of every nephron is a cup-like collector called the Bowman's capsule. This surrounds a knot of blood capillaries (photo far right). Hundreds of cup-and-knot pairs are packed into the outer cortex of a kidney (right).

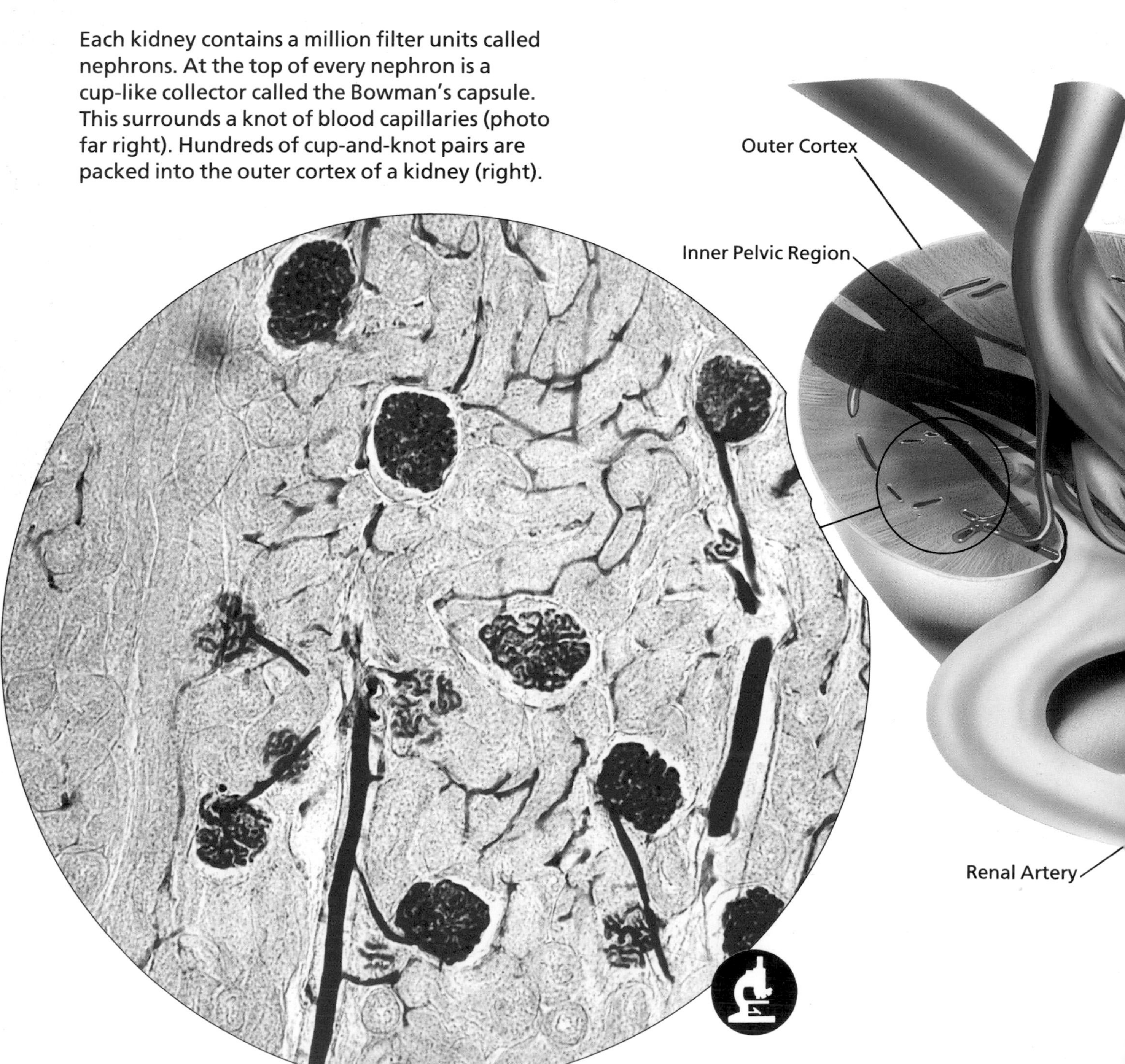

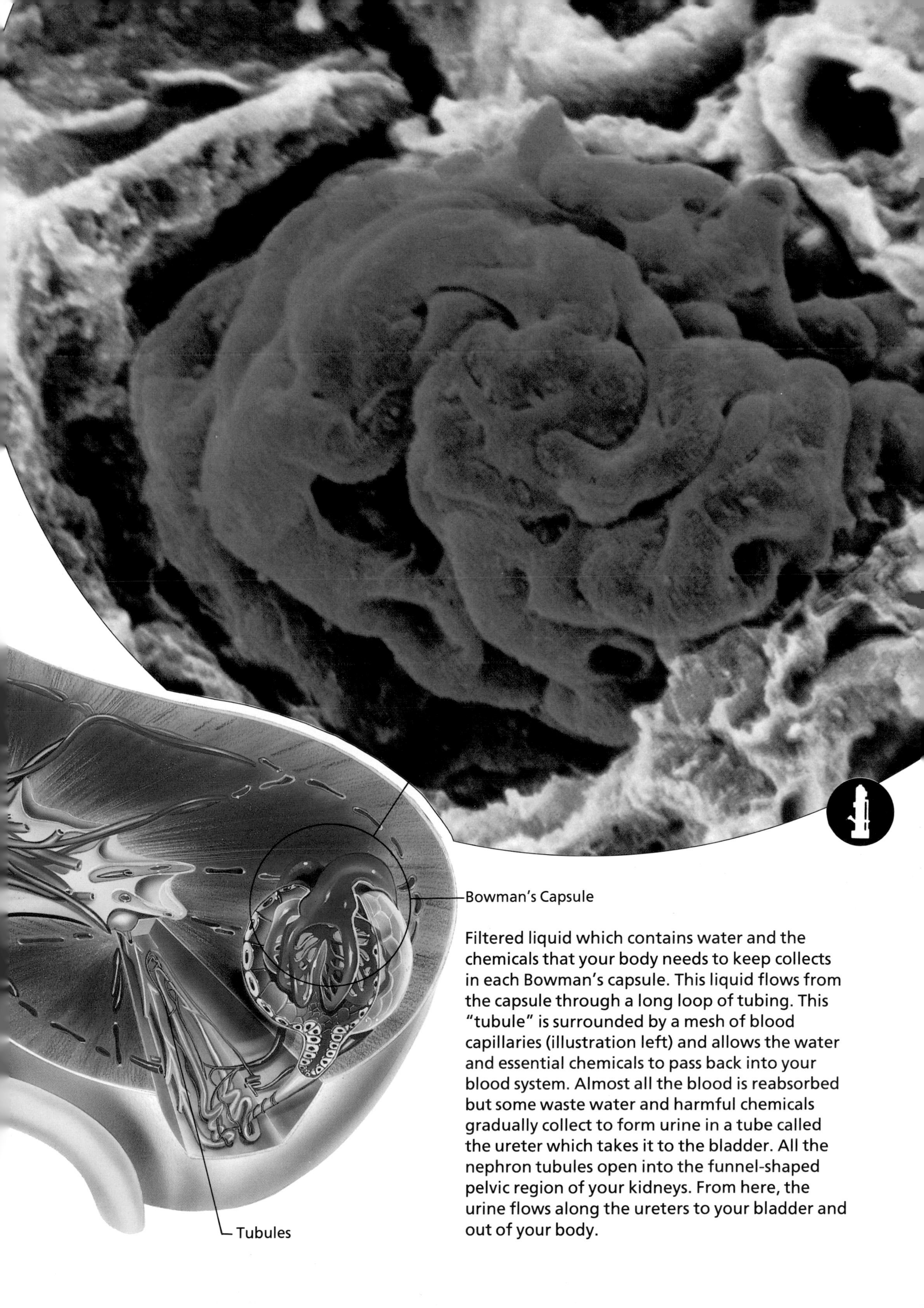

Filtered liquid which contains water and the chemicals that your body needs to keep collects in each Bowman's capsule. This liquid flows from the capsule through a long loop of tubing. This "tubule" is surrounded by a mesh of blood capillaries (illustration left) and allows the water and essential chemicals to pass back into your blood system. Almost all the blood is reabsorbed but some waste water and harmful chemicals gradually collect to form urine in a tube called the ureter which takes it to the bladder. All the nephron tubules open into the funnel-shaped pelvic region of your kidneys. From here, the urine flows along the ureters to your bladder and out of your body.

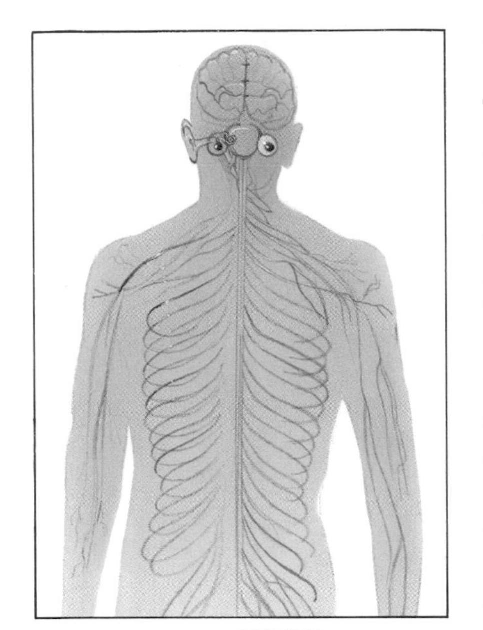

THE NERVOUS SYSTEM

Your body has a communication and control network called the nervous system. Its headquarters is the brain where 12,000 million cells are constantly sending and receiving messages. Tiny nerve fibers act like telephone wires and carry signals throughout the body. Some of these fibers branch out from the base of the brain, others from your spinal cord. Information about our surroundings is sent to the brain from our sense organs (the nose, eyes, ears and tongue), as well as from the nerves embedded in our skin and muscles. The brain receives all the information and decides how we should act. All the pictures on these two pages show details of the brain and your body's nervous system.

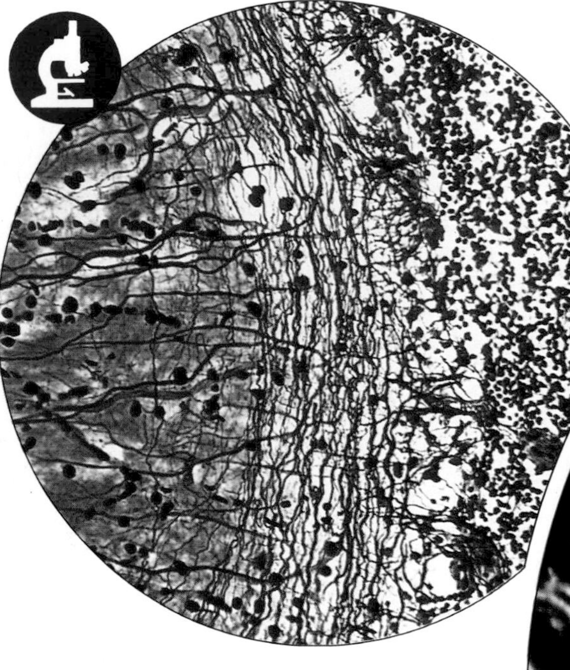

A view through the very folded outer layers of the brain (above) shows a tightly packed area of nerve cells. Each is connected to thousands of others by tree-like "dendrites" (see illustration far right). These form a mass of strands which carry messages or "nerve impulses" – short bursts of electricity. The dendrites are so densely packed in the brain that they resemble the wires of a complicated telephone exchange. Millions of signals pass along them every minute, which the brain decodes as hot or cold, soft or hard, for example.

The picture below is an electron microscope's view of a synapse, a junction between two nerve fibers in the outer part of a human brain. The colors are false, the brain is in fact gray.

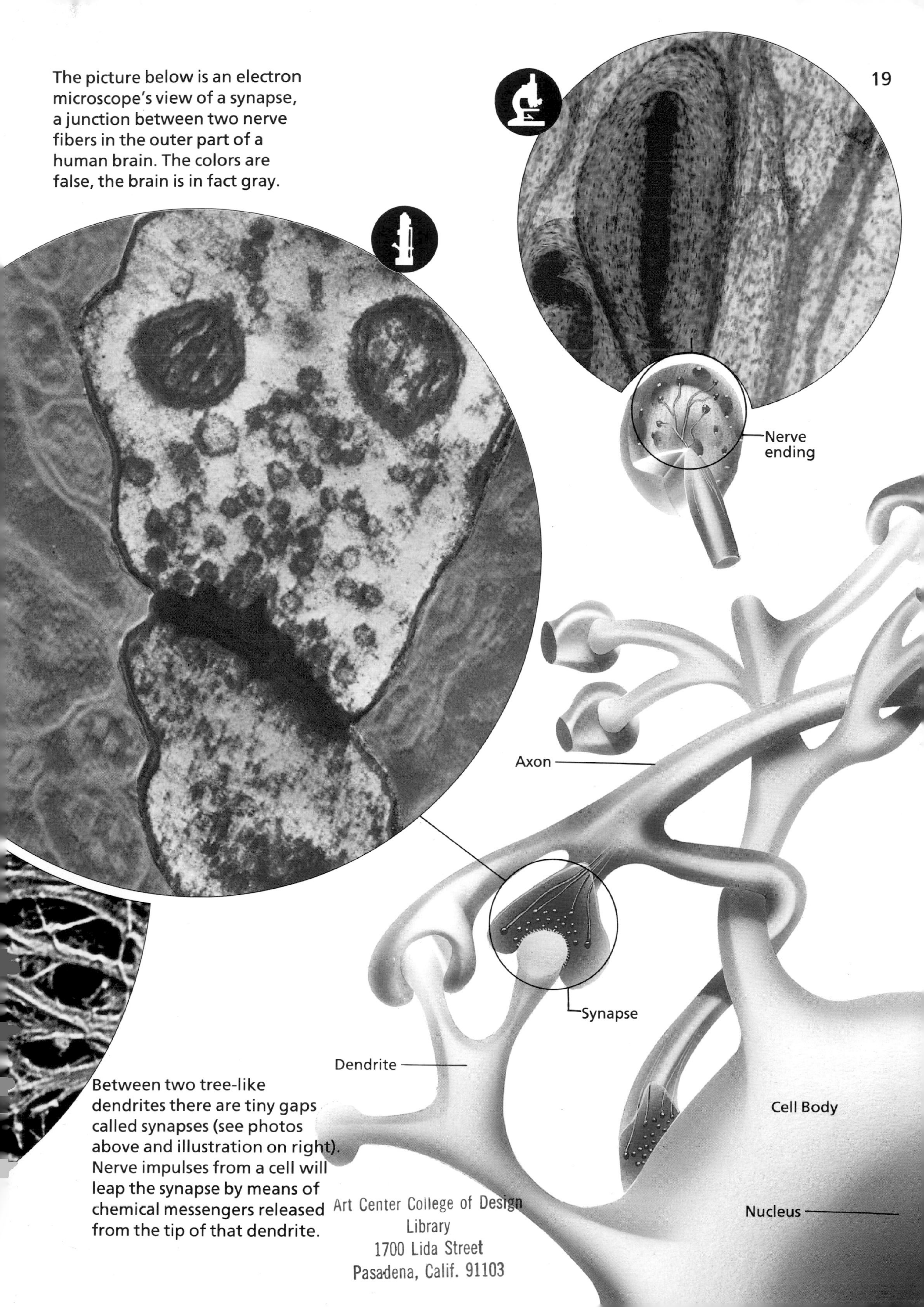

Between two tree-like dendrites there are tiny gaps called synapses (see photos above and illustration on right). Nerve impulses from a cell will leap the synapse by means of chemical messengers released from the tip of that dendrite.

EYES AND EARS

The five senses are touch, taste, smell, sight and hearing. Each makes us aware of our surroundings by using microscopic nerve cells. Just as your skin has nerves which are sensitive to hot and cold (see pages 6 & 7) so we see, hear, smell and taste with groups of cells called receptors. Their special job is to report changes to the nerves they are attached to. In our eyes these work by noticing changes in the light falling on them. In our ears receptors sense changes in sound. Receptors operate our sense of smell in the same way, by sending nerve signals to our brains to be interpreted. For example, our eyes see upside down but the brain decodes this information so that we know which is the right way up.

Each of your eyes is like a miniature camera. At the front is a clear, curved window called the cornea. The colored area, the iris, see picture on the right, is a ring of muscle that controls the amount of light shining on the lens . This lens forms a sharp picture on receptor cells within the retina at the back of the eye. These signal the brain via the optic nerve (see illustration below), so that the optic nerve carries a picture to the brain where it can be studied.

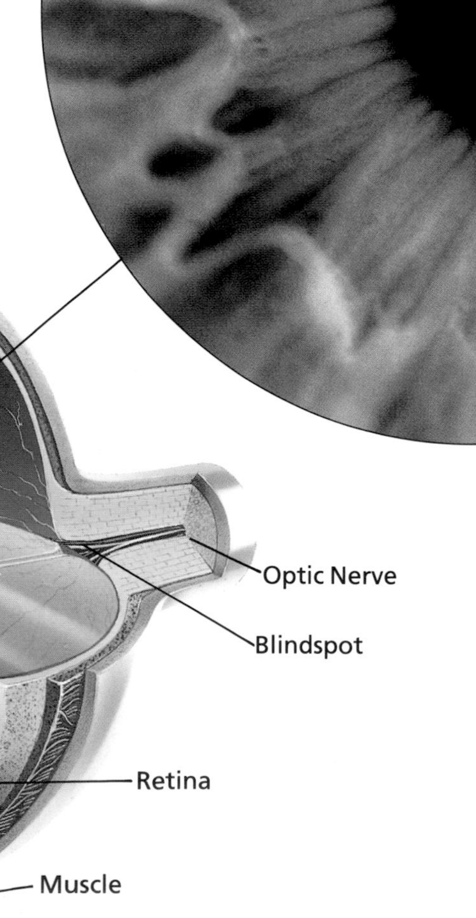

There are more than 130 million light receptors in the retina. They are arranged like nerve cells in the brain and are linked to one another. Most of these receptors simply detect changes in the levels of light. The rest are sensitive to color and allow your brain to build up information which will produce a realistic image of what is being viewed.

Sounds are really vibrations in the air. The outer ear, or pinna, funnels these down the bony canal to the ear-drum which trembles and moves three connected earbones in the middle ear. They pass vibrations to the inner ear where the cochlea, or hearing organ, a shell-like tube, receives them. Within it are receptors with hairs sticking into a jelly-like mass (see below right). Sounds make fluid in the cochlea move and cause the hairs to send signals to your brain along the auditory nerve.

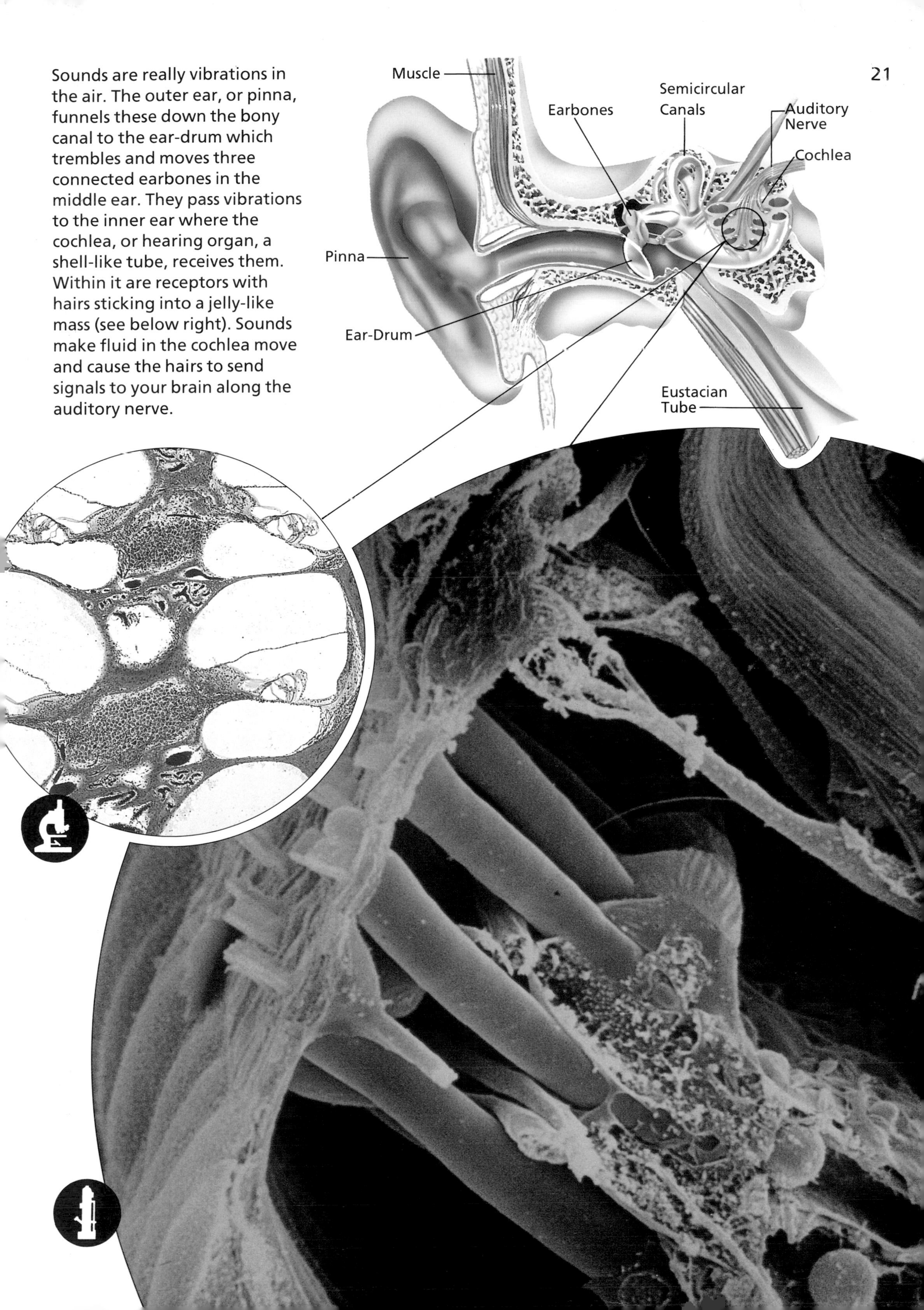

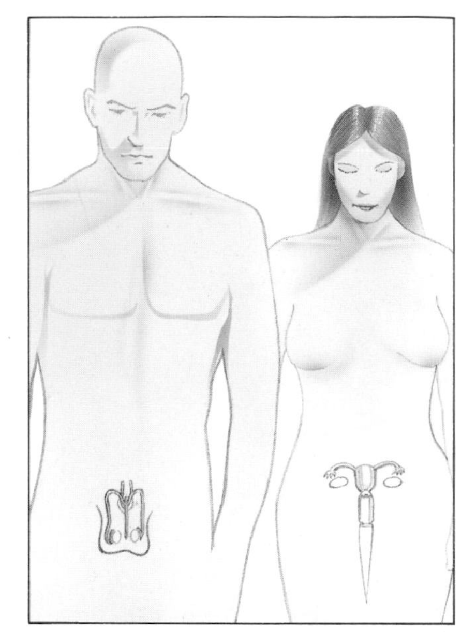

THE REPRODUCTIVE SYSTEM

Human life goes on because we are able to produce more humans like ourselves. This is called reproduction and every sex plays its part. An adult male produces about 200 million seed-cells, or sperm, in his testes every day. Sperm are so tiny that several hundred would easily fit onto a pin-head. A female's ovaries make one egg-cell, or ovum, each month. The ovum is the largest human cell and is just visible to the naked eye. Despite their minute sizes, a sperm and an ovum together contain all the information needed to produce a new human being. Following sexual intercourse, millions of sperm come into contact with an ovum. But just one sperm combines with, or fertilizes, the ovum to make an embryo.

The testicles, a cross-section of one is illustrated below, are two sperm-making organs attached to a male body.

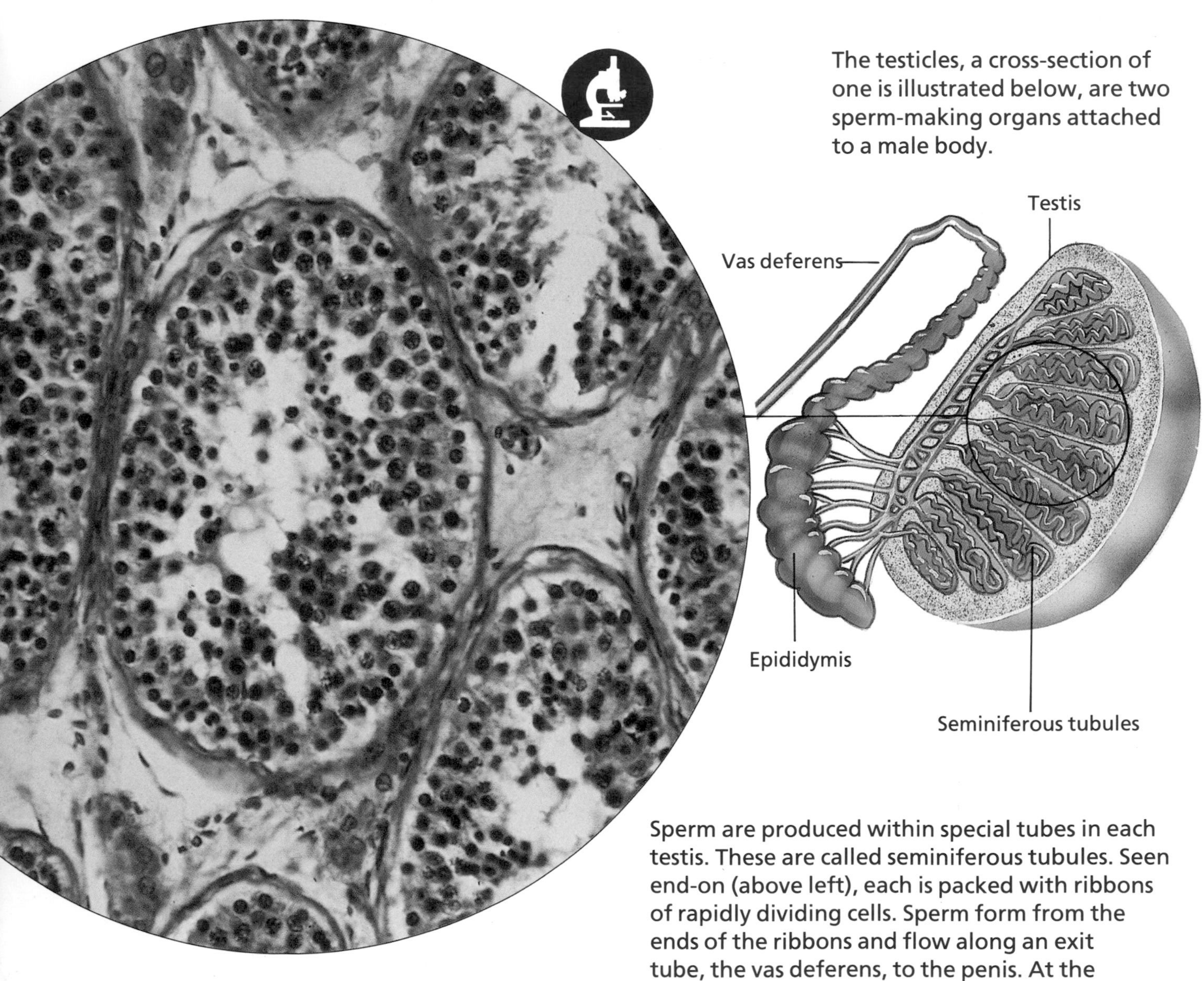

Sperm are produced within special tubes in each testis. These are called seminiferous tubules. Seen end-on (above left), each is packed with ribbons of rapidly dividing cells. Sperm form from the ends of the ribbons and flow along an exit tube, the vas deferens, to the penis. At the climax of sexual intercourse, called an orgasm, the sperm are ejaculated by the penis and millions of them swim off to try and fertilize the woman's ovum.

At any one moment, there are cells at different stages of development in each of a woman's two ovaries (see photo right). When these become mature ovum they are released into the fallopian tubes (see below left). The ovum is pushed toward the womb by muscles in the wall of this tube. Along the way it may encounter sperm which have swum up from the vagina. Cells lining the walls of the ovum sac produce chemicals called hormones to control this entire process. Once an ovum is fertilized by a single sperm the egg divides and its cells begin to multiply. Within three weeks it will become an embryo, and after nine months a baby will be born, if all goes well.

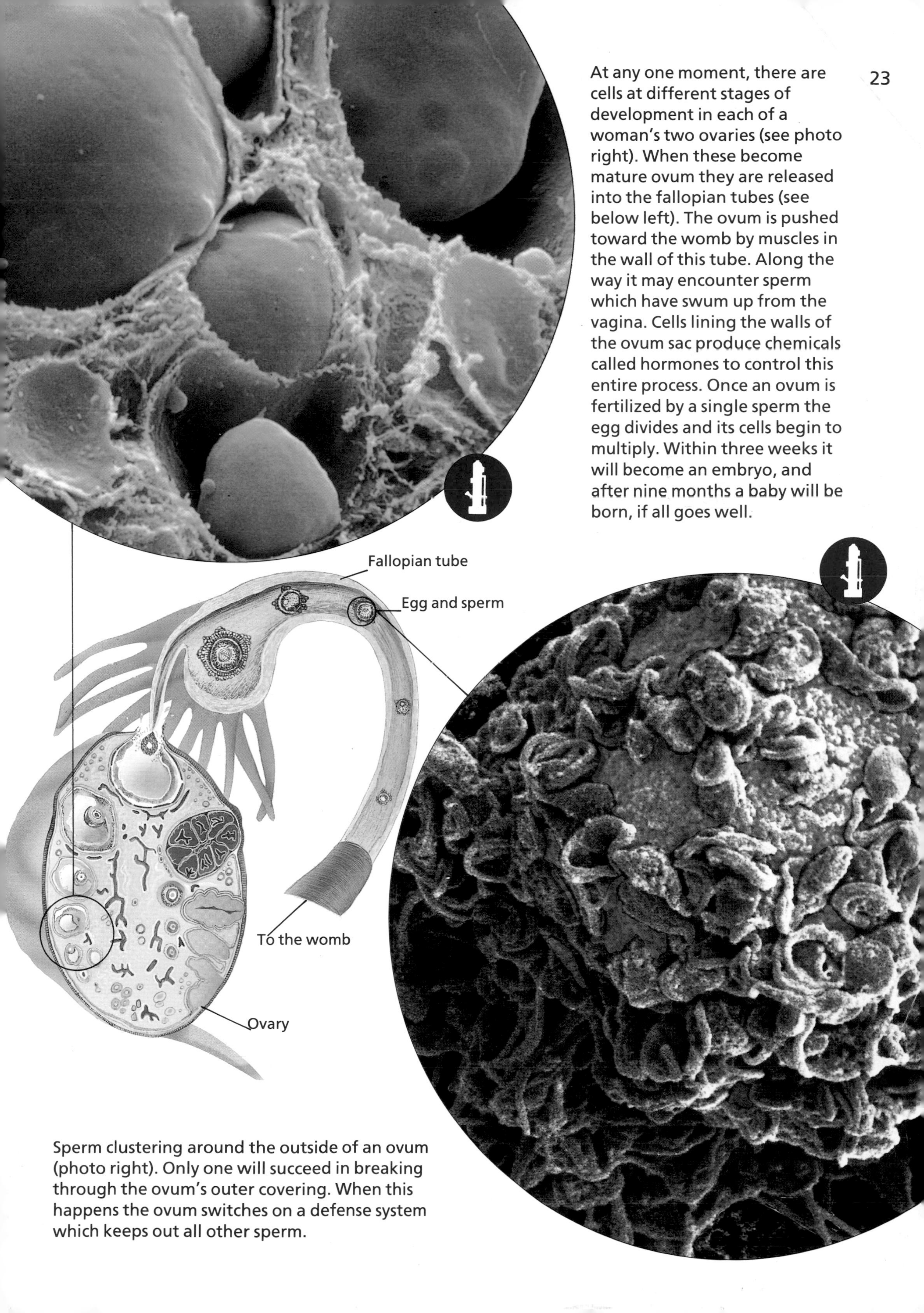

Sperm clustering around the outside of an ovum (photo right). Only one will succeed in breaking through the ovum's outer covering. When this happens the ovum switches on a defense system which keeps out all other sperm.

THE EMBRYO

No matter how different we all look from one another, we all started life in our mother's body as a ball of cells less than 1mm (1⁄16 in) wide. This ball, or blastocyst, was formed by the fertilized egg dividing four or five times. With some 30 more cell divisions, the blastocyst develops into an embryo, or growing baby. Only seven weeks after a sperm and ovum joined together the embryo measures about 25mm (one in) long. Most parts of its body are formed and working. The embryo receives food and oxygen from the placenta. This is an organ that develops in the womb and is connected to the embryo by the umbilical cord. Nine months after fertilization, the baby is ready to leave the mother's body.

The blastocyst is made up of about 100 cells arranged as an outer ring and an inner mass. But soon different types of cells – nerve, muscle, blood and digestive – start to develop.

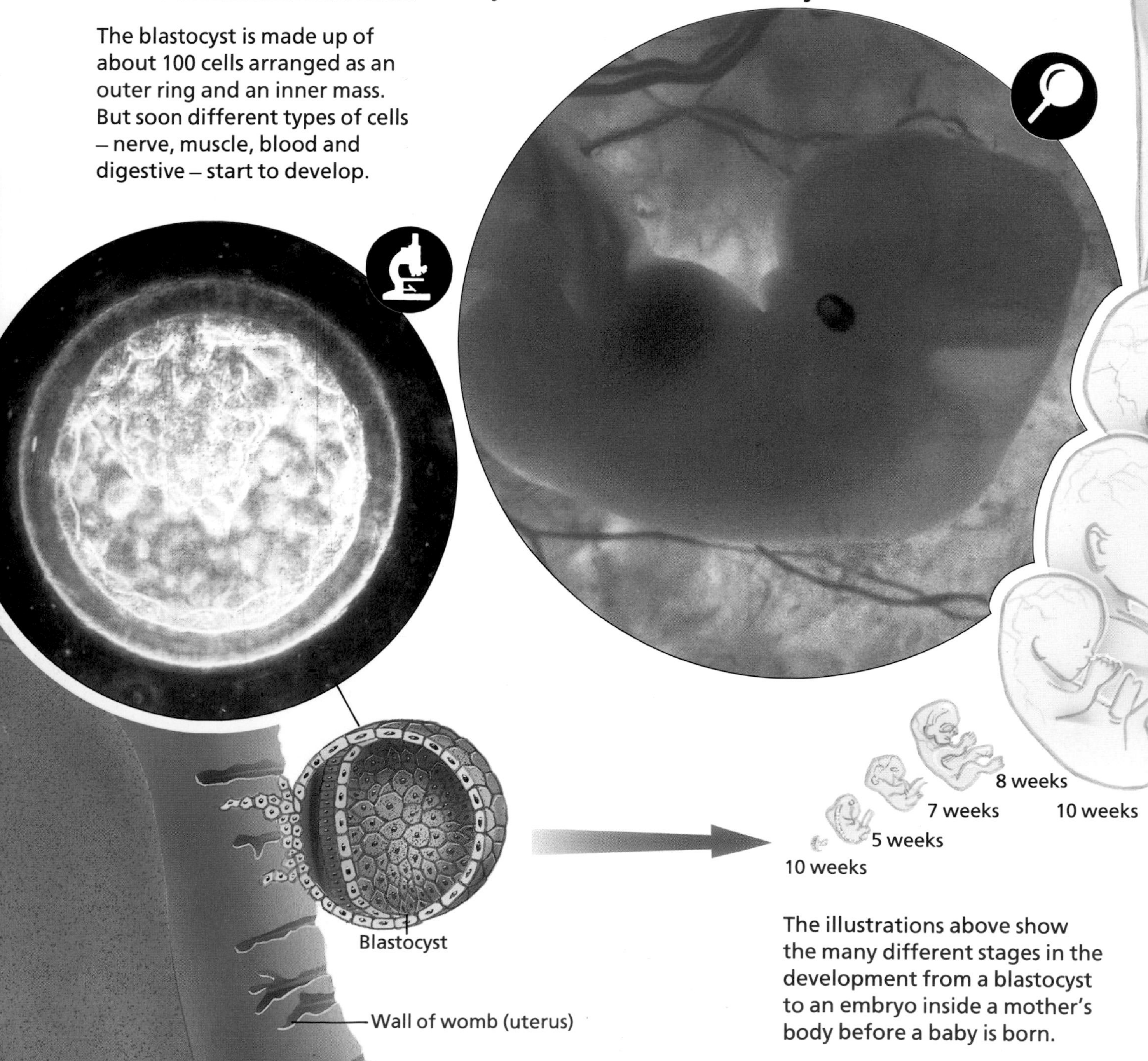

The illustrations above show the many different stages in the development from a blastocyst to an embryo inside a mother's body before a baby is born.

A fertilized ovum, called a zygote, travels slowly down the fallopian tube dividing so that when it reaches the uterus 7 days later it consists of many hundreds of cells. On arrival in the uterus it attacks the walls, digesting its cells and burrowing-in until it is firmly attached. After only 3 weeks the basic plan of the body has developed – the head, the skin, the digestive tube, muscle and bone are all in place. By 7 weeks, the embryo has arms and legs and looks like a tiny person (photo below). After 5 months, the infant is 30cm (1 ft) long from top to toe and weighs 681g (1½ lbs). It can now grip with its hands, wriggle its toes, and open and close its eyelids. At the age of 9 months it consists of 20,000 million cells, measures 50cm (20 in) long and weighs 3.3kg (7 lbs).

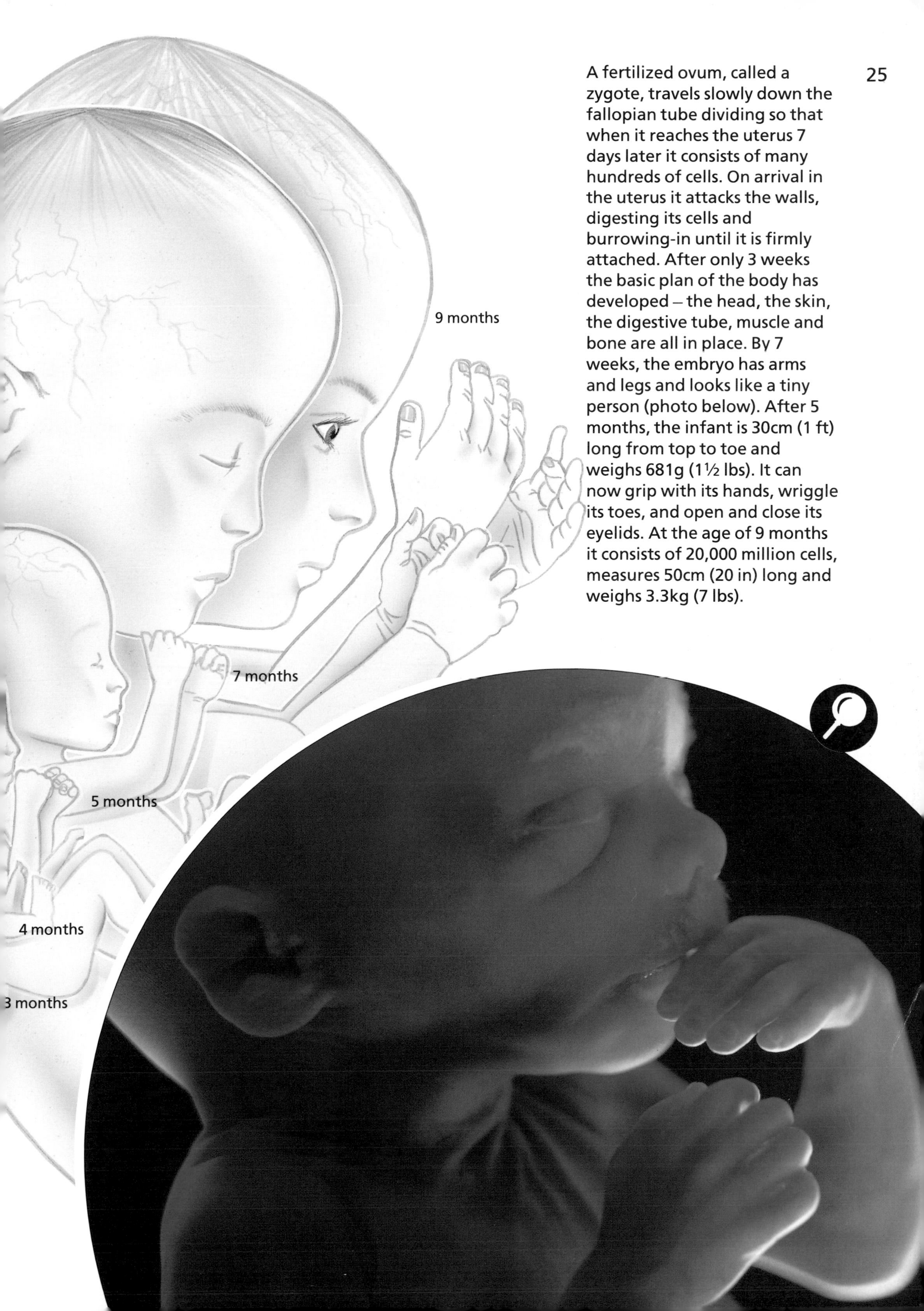

BODY DEFENSES AND ATTACKERS

Your body is under constant attack by microscopic creatures. They live in the air we breathe, the water we drink, and the food we eat. Many of these germs can make you sick or harm your body if they grow and breed inside of you. Poisons can enter your bloodstream if you are bitten by an animal, or cut yourself with a rusty nail. But your body has many defenses. For example, dust and germs are trapped in nose-hairs when you breathe; and chemicals in the digestive system destroy most invaders. There are even special cells in the bloodstream and lymphatic system which battle any attackers they come across.

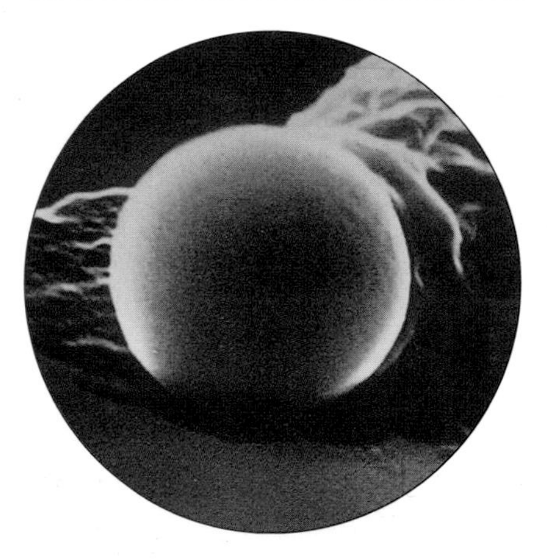

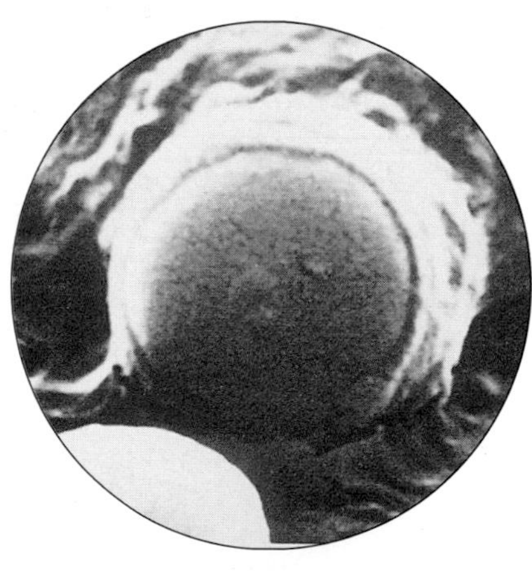

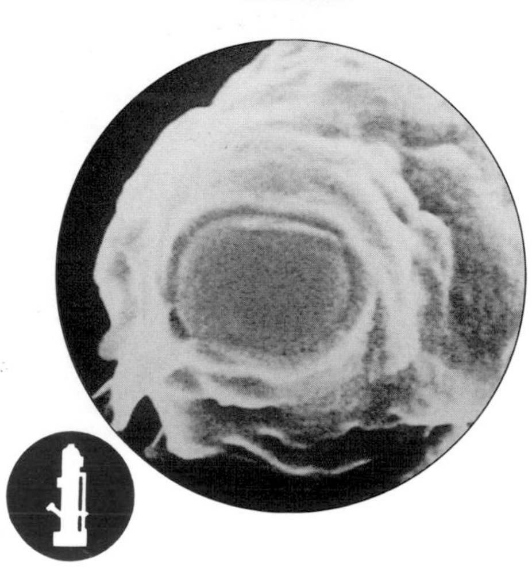

White blood cells act as hunter-killers in your body. They gobble up and destroy bacteria by flowing around and then digesting them. Sometimes, however, poisons produced by the bacteria kill the white blood cells first. During blood transfusions red blood cells are taken from one person (the donor) and given to another (the recipient). If the people's bloods do not mix, the recipient's white cells treat the donor's red cells as if they were bacteria, and destroy them (photos left show this in stages).

Much of your food contains bacteria and some may carry the larval form or resting stage of parasites, which are creatures that can live inside your body. Usually, all of these are killed during cooking. Tapeworms are about 1cm (almost ½ inch) wide and can grow to 10m (33 feet) in length, and develop from tiny larvae found in uncooked meat. The head of the worm burrows into the wall of the intestine and hangs on with suckers and hooks (right). Tapeworms will feed off of the nutrients we bring into our bodies as food. If not removed, they can make people very ill.

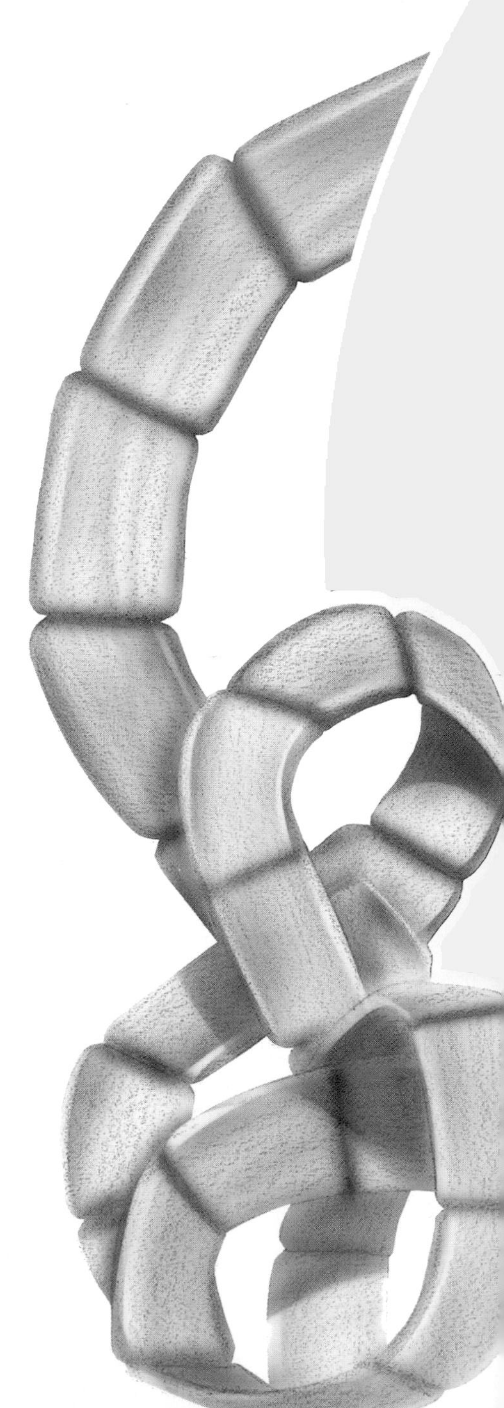

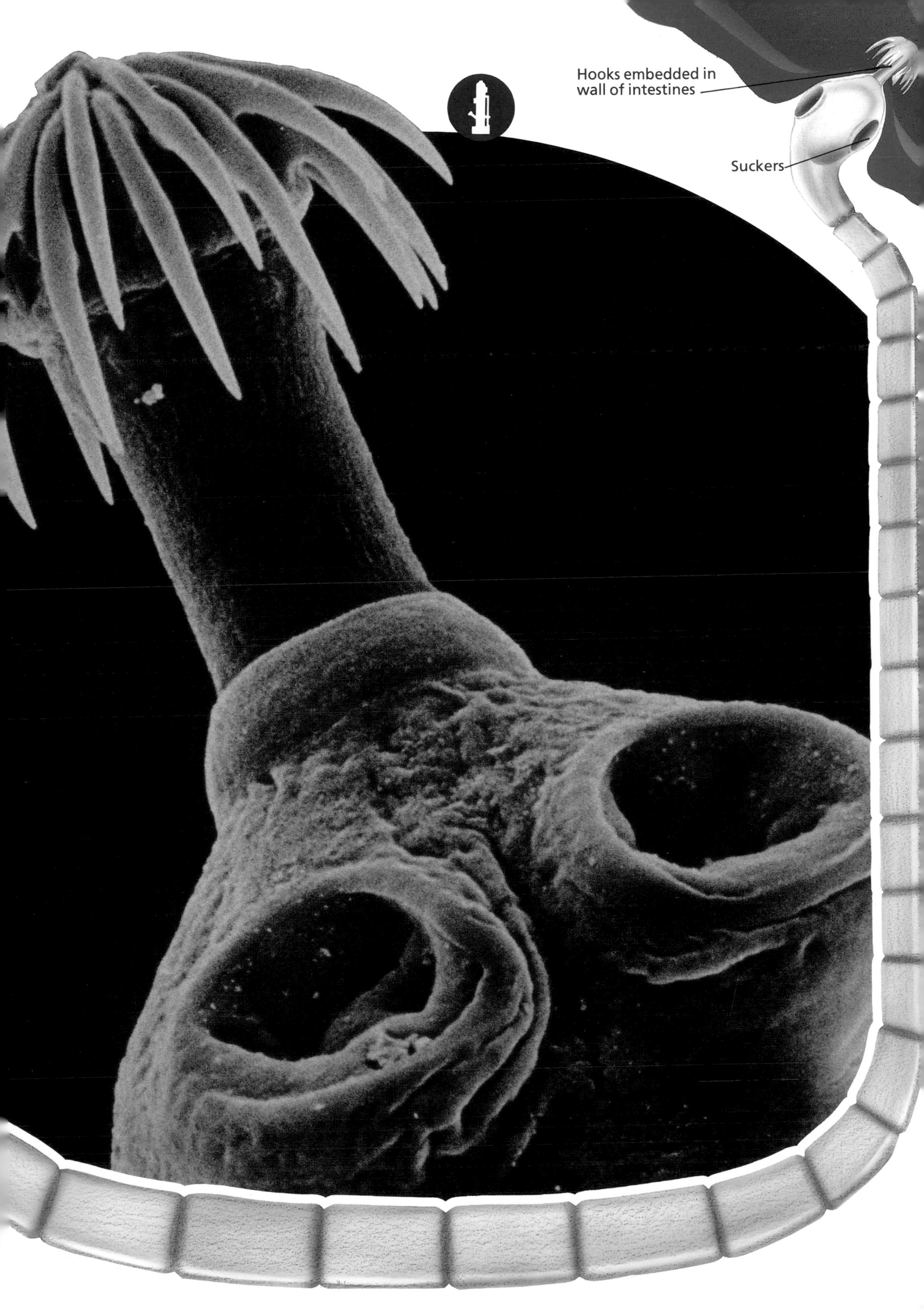
Hooks embedded in wall of intestines
Suckers

PRACTICAL PROJECTS

You can discover a great deal about nature's miniature world with just a magnifying glass. But to see the detailed structure of tissues and organs, you will need a microscope like the one shown on page 4. The objects you want to study must be mounted on a glass slide. They must also be made very thin so that light can shine through them. To distinguish all the different types of cells, you will need to stain your specimens with special dyes. Below, we outline how this can be done. However, making good microscope slides may call for some help from an experienced adult. Start your studies with some ready-made slides bought from a microscope supplier, and try out the simple projects shown opposite.

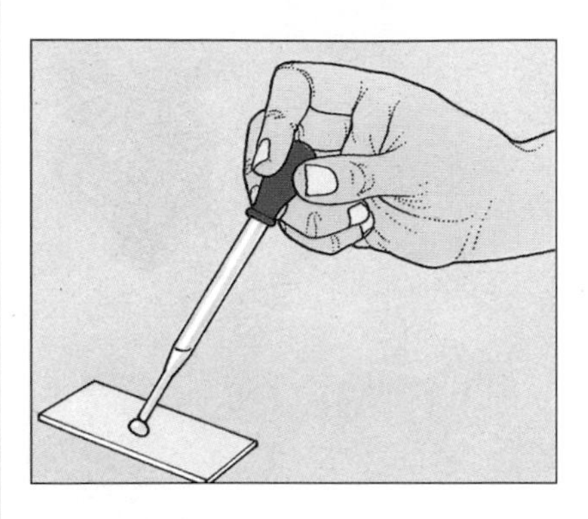

To prepare a cell slide, place a drop of clean water containing the cells on the glass slide.

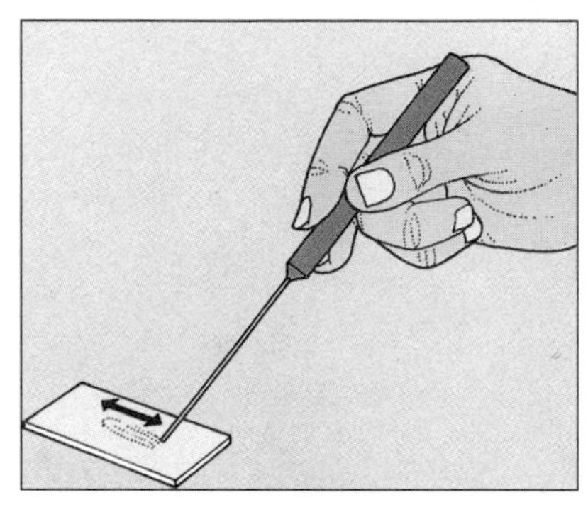

With a wire loop that has been sterilized in a flame, spread the fluid thinly and let it dry.

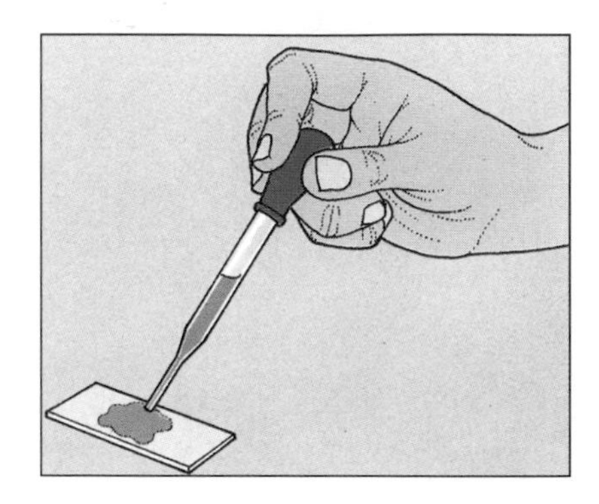

Add a small drop of staining dye to the cells and leave for a few minutes.

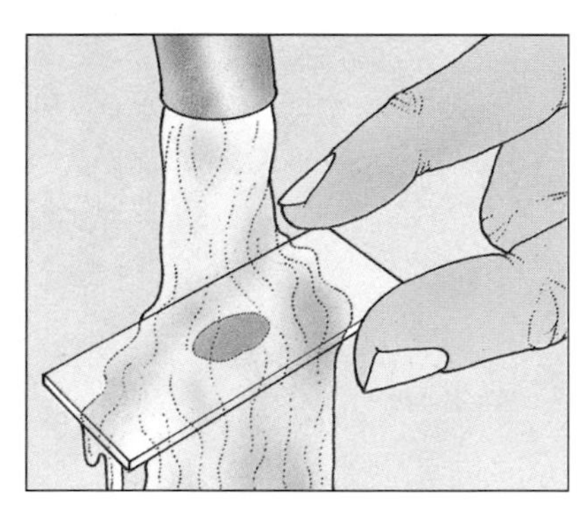

Wash off the dye with water or alcohol. You can stain with another, contrasting dye.

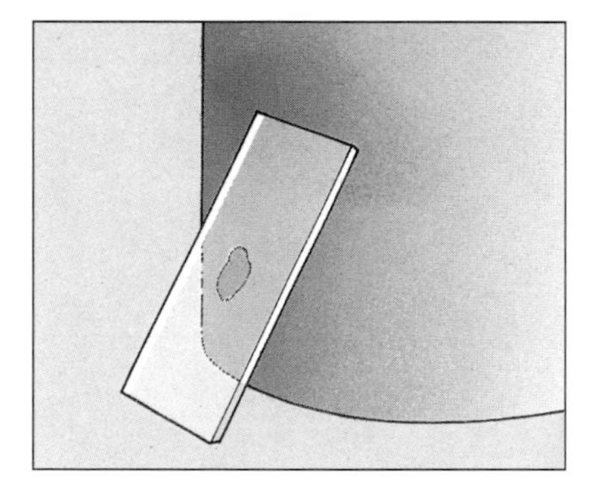

Leave the slide to dry. You can speed up drying by gently warming the slide over a flame.

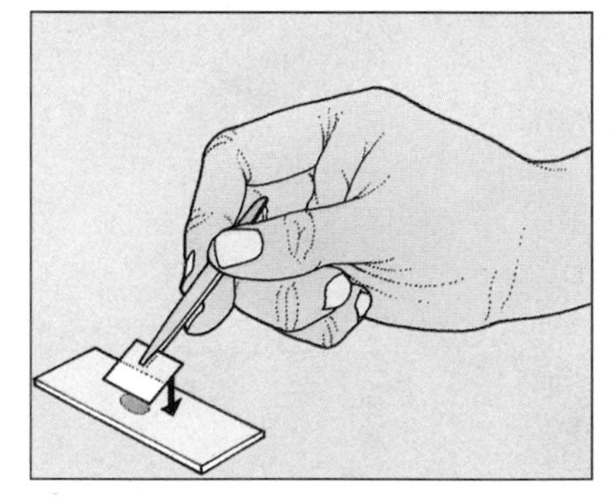

Place a cover slip (a thin square of glass) over the stained cells, using a pair of tweezers.

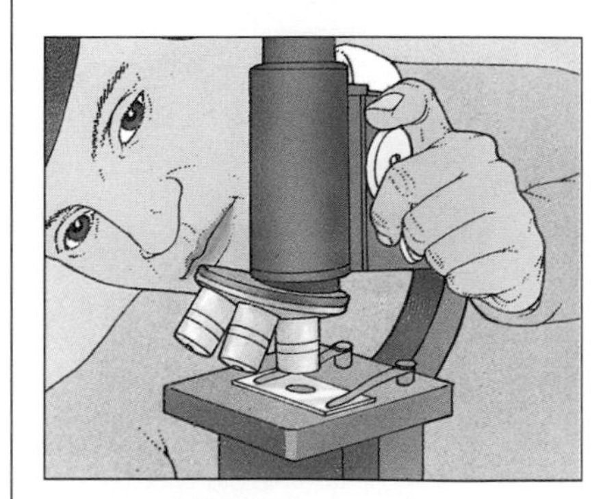

Put the slide on the microscope stage and position the mirror to give you good illumination.

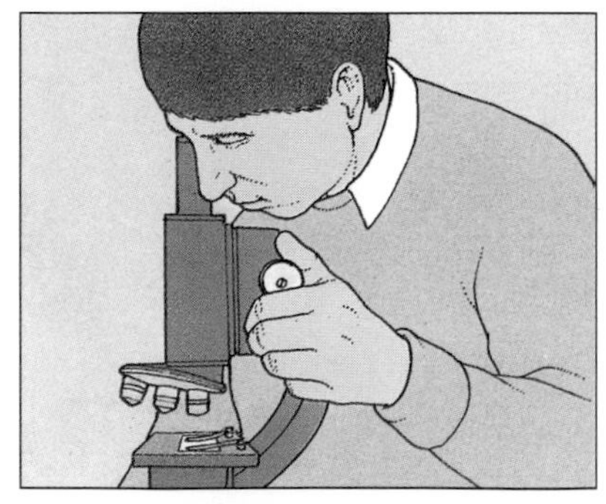

Select the objective lens you want, then move the eyepiece up and down to focus. Start at the lowest magnification.

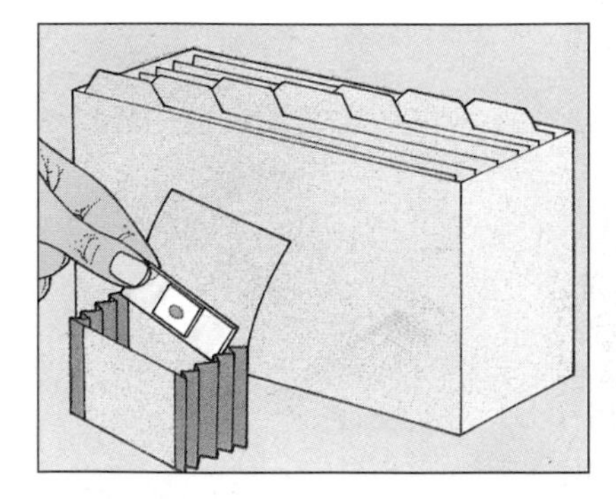

Keep your prepared slides in a wallet made from a folded sheet of thin cardboard, which will protect them from dust.

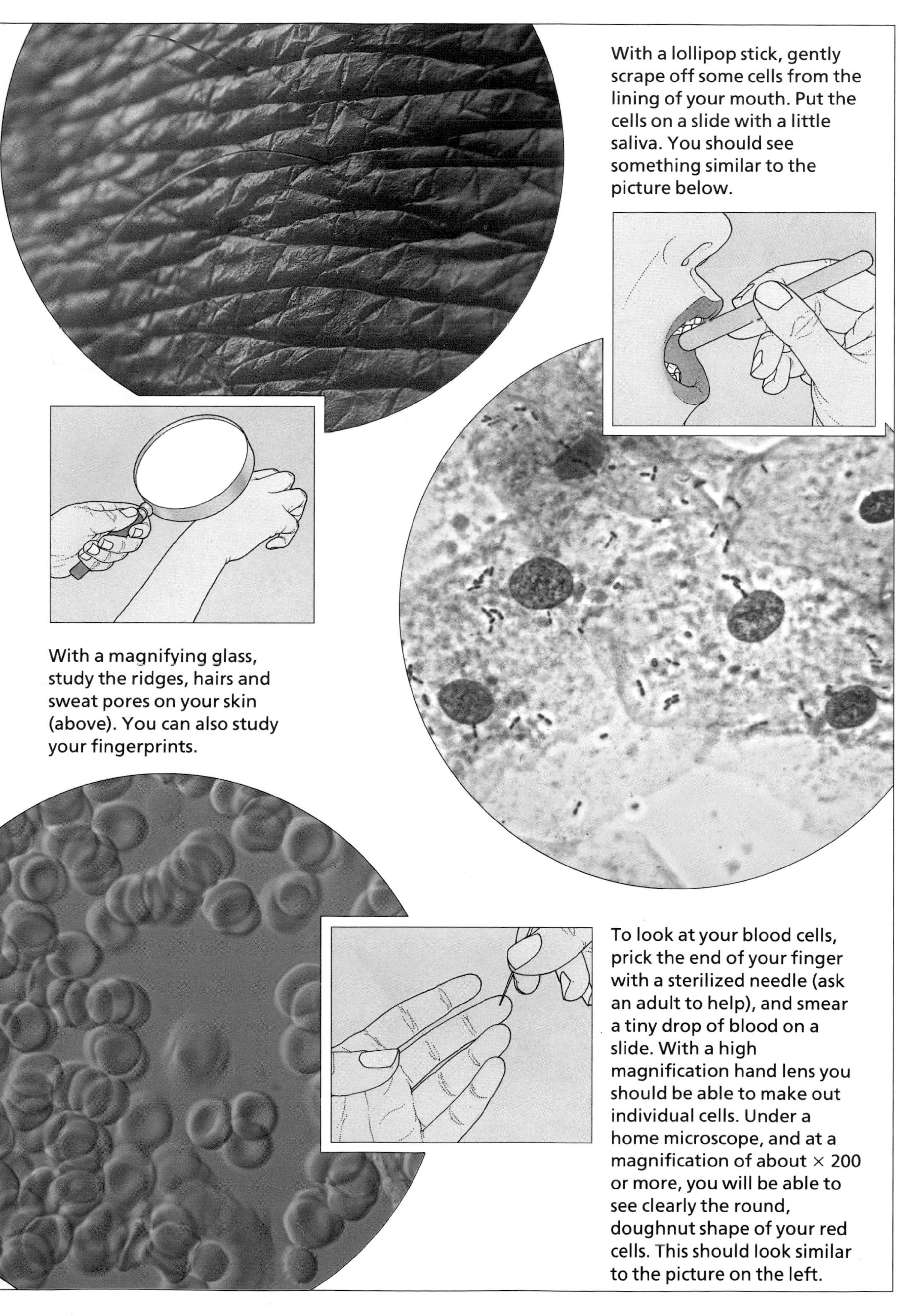

With a lollipop stick, gently scrape off some cells from the lining of your mouth. Put the cells on a slide with a little saliva. You should see something similar to the picture below.

With a magnifying glass, study the ridges, hairs and sweat pores on your skin (above). You can also study your fingerprints.

To look at your blood cells, prick the end of your finger with a sterilized needle (ask an adult to help), and smear a tiny drop of blood on a slide. With a high magnification hand lens you should be able to make out individual cells. Under a home microscope, and at a magnification of about $\times$ 200 or more, you will be able to see clearly the round, doughnut shape of your red cells. This should look similar to the picture on the left.

MICROPHOTOGRAPHY

All of the high magnification photographs shown in this book were taken by fitting a camera to the eyepiece section of a scientific microscope. These pictures are known as microphotographs. The colors in them are not natural, but are produced either by staining the tissue or organ samples or by coloring the images using computer graphics to highlight different features.

If you have a home microscope, you can take your own microphotographs. You will need a single-lens reflex camera and a special camera attachment. On the other hand, many of the close-up pictures in this book were taken with extension rings and bellows fitted to a single-lens reflex camera. These can magnify even more than a hand-lens and give some very impressive results.

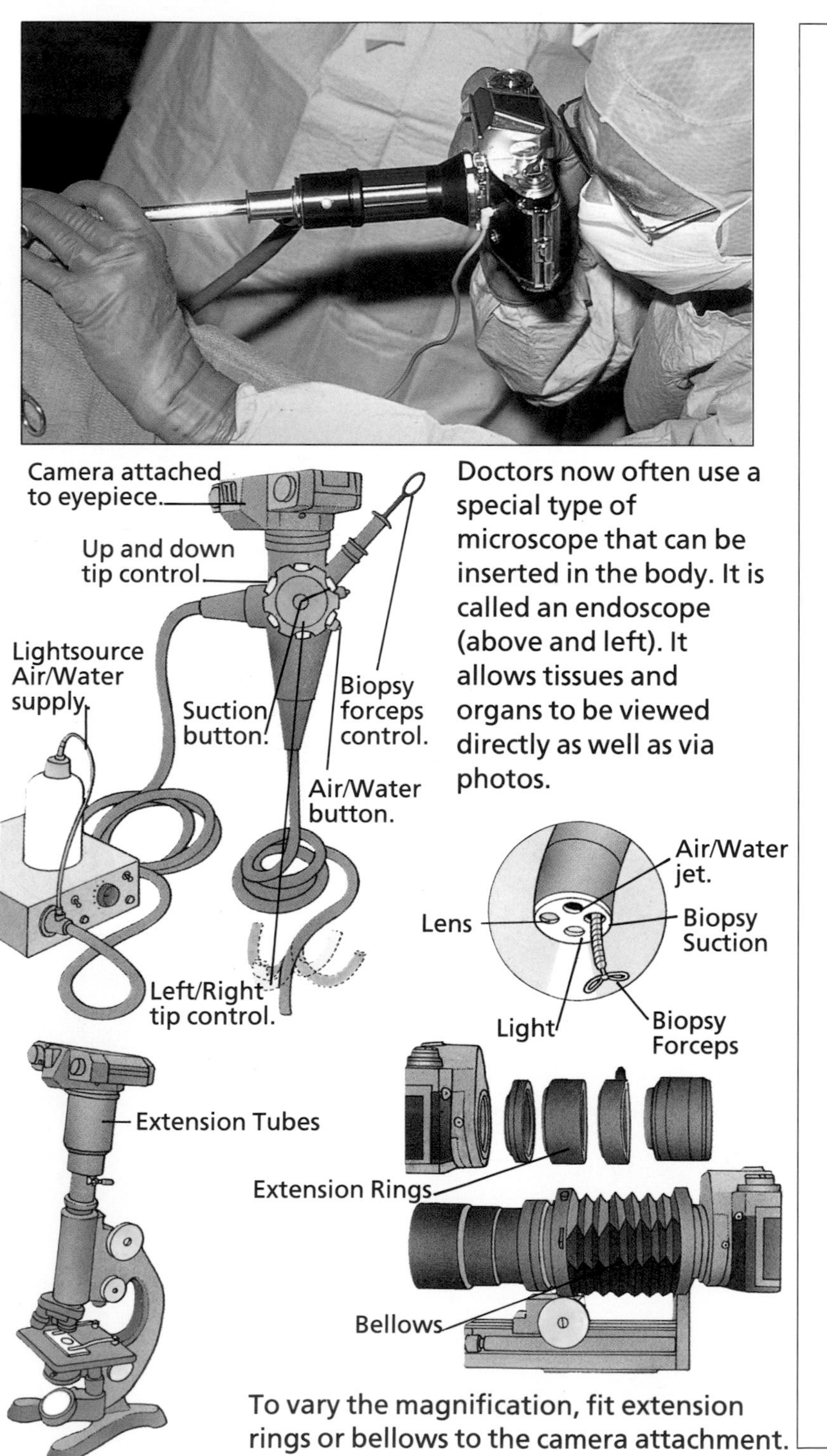

Doctors now often use a special type of microscope that can be inserted in the body. It is called an endoscope (above and left). It allows tissues and organs to be viewed directly as well as via photos.

To vary the magnification, fit extension rings or bellows to the camera attachment.

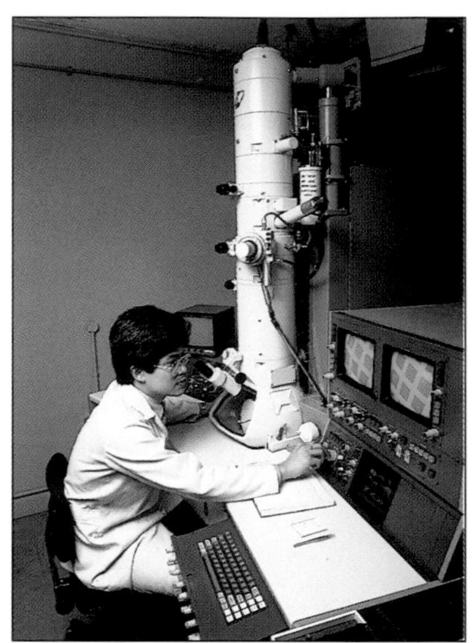

There are two main types of electron microscope. In a transmission type (TEM), a beam of electrons is passed through an extemely thin slice of tissue and an image is produced on a viewing screen. On a scanning electron microscope an (SEM), a fine beam of electrons is moved across the surface of the tissue for reflections to be collected and used to create an image on a television type of screen. Using an SEM, realistic 3-D images are produced. But as with all types of microscope specimens, the tissues and organs are no longer alive. The slide preparation process kills live cells. The colors on photos produced using an SEM are false colors added in processing.

GLOSSARY:

blood a red fluid that travels around the body in the veins and arteries. Blood is made up of the plasma, a straw colored liquid in which float red and white corpuscles.

bone the tissue that forms the skeleton of the human body.

brain the organ within the skull which coordinates and controls the body; the headquarters of the nervous system.

capillaries microscopic blood vessels; tubes which carry blood to every cell in the body.

carbon dioxide one of the body's waste products; it is released by the cells into the bloodstream during the chemical breakdown of food, and passed out of the body as a gas.

cell the smallest unit or building block of living things. Most cells in the human body are about 0.03mm (0.001) across and can be seen only with a microscope. Each cell consists of an outer skin, or membrane, surrounding a jelly-like material made up of water and chemicals called proteins.

dermis the lower layer of skin on a human body.

digestive system the body's food processing system, which includes the mouth, pharynx, esophagus, stomach and the small and large intestines. It is also known as the alimentary system or sometimes as the "guts."

epidermis the upper layer of skin on a human body.

heart the muscular organ which acts like a double pump to push blood into the lungs and around the body. It is situated between the lungs, slightly left of center in the chest.

hormones the body's chemical messengers. They flow around the blood system and control tissue growth and development.

magnification the number of times the diameter, or distance across, something appears enlarged or made bigger.

nerve a bundle of fibers that carry information between the brain and parts of the body.

neuron a nerve cell. It consists of a long thin fiber and many short tree-like projections called the dendrites.

organ a major part of the body such as the heart, lungs, eyes, ears, or kidneys. Organs are made of one or more types of tissue and each has a particular job to do.

oxygen the gas needed by our body's cells to convert food into energy.

tissue a collection of cells of the same type.

WEIGHTS AND MEASURES

mm = millimeter 10mm = 1cm = 4/10 inch
cm = centimeter 100cm = 1m = 3 1/3 feet
m = meter 1,000m = 1km = 6/10 mile
km = kilometer
lb = pound g = gram 1,000g = 1kg = 2lb 3 ounces
kg = kilogram

0.1 = 1/10
0.01 = 1/100
0.001 = 1/1,000

INDEX

alveoli 12, 13
aorta 10,11
arteries 10
arterioles 10

bacteria 26
bladder 17
blastocyst 24, 25
blood 10, 11, 12, 14, 16, 27, 29 31
blood system 14, 26
blood vessels 7, 8, 9, 10
bones 8, 9, 25, 31
Bowman's capsule 16, 17
brain 8, 12, 18, 20, 31
bronchioles 12, 13

capillaries 8, 12, 13, 15, 16, 17, 31
cells 5, 6, 7, 9, 10, 12, 16, 22, 23, 24, 29, 31
cochlea 21
cornea 20
corpuscles 10, 31

dendrites 18, 19
dermis 6, 7, 31
digestive system 14, 15, 26, 31

elbow 8
embryo 22, 24, 25
endoscope 30
epidermis 6, 7, 31

fallopian tube 23
feet 6
fibers, muscle 8
fingerprint 6
fingers 6
follicles 7
food 9, 14, 16, 24, 26

germs 6, 10, 12

heart 11, 16, 31
hormones 10, 23, 31

intestines 14, 15
iris 20

joints 8

keratin 7
kidneys 10, 16
knee 8

legs 9, 25
lenses 4, 20
liver 10, 15
lungs 10, 12, 13
lymph system 14, 15, 26

magnification 4, 5, 31
microscopes, types of 4, 30
minerals 16
mouth 14, 29
mucus 12
muscles 8, 11, 18, 20, 23, 25

nerve cells (neurons) 14, 18, 20, 31
nerve fibers 18
nerve impulses 18, 19
nerves 7, 8, 31
nervous system 18
nose 20

optic nerve 20
organs 10, 28, 31
ovaries 22, 23
ovum 22, 23, 24
oxygen 9, 10, 12, 24, 31

penis 22
placenta 24
plasma 10, 31

receptors 20, 21
reproductive system 22
respiratory system 26

seminiferous tubule 22
senses 18, 19, 20, 21
skin 6, 7, 19, 20, 25, 26
sperm 22, 23, 24
spinal cord 18
stomach 14, 15
sweat glands 7
sweat pore 7
synapse 19

tapeworm 26
taste buds 14
testes 22
tissues 5, 6, 8, 9, 10, 28, 31
tongue 14, 19, 20
trachea 12
tubule 17

umbilical cord 24
urea 10
ureters 17
uterus 24, 25

valve, mitral 11
vas deferens 22
veins 10
ventricles 11

waste materials 9, 10, 16
water 12, 16, 17, 26
womb 23, 24

Photographic Credits:
Cover and pages 6, 7, 8, 9, 10, 11, 12, 13t, 14, 17, 18, 19, 20, 21, 22, 23, 24r, 25, 26, 27, 29t and m and 30: Science Photo Library; pages 13b, 15, 16, 24l and 29b: Biophoto Associates.